At Issue

Populism in the Digital Age

Other Books in the At Issue Series

At Issue

| Populism in the
| Digital Age

Anne Cunningham, Book Editor

GREENHAVEN
PUBLISHING

Published in 2018 by Greenhaven Publishing, LLC
353 3rd Avenue, Suite 255, New York, NY 10010

Articles in Greenhaven Publishing anthologies are often edited for length to meet page
requirements. In addition, original titles of these works are changed to clearly present
the main thesis and to explicitly indicate the author's opinion. Every effort is made to
ensure that Greenhaven Publishing accurately reflects the original intent of the authors.
Every effort has been made to trace the owners of the copyrighted material.

Cover image: Arthimedes/Shutterstock.com

Cataloging-in-Publication Data

Names: Cunningham, Anne, editor.
Title: Populism in the digital age / edited by Anne Cunningham.
Description: New York : Greenhaven Publishing, 2018. | Series: At issue |
Includes bibliographical references and index. | Audience: Grades 9-12.
Identifiers: LCCN ISBN 9781534502079 (library bound) | ISBN 9781534502147 (pbk.)
Subjects: LCSH: Communication in politics--Juvenile literature.
| Political science--Philosophy--Juvenile literature.
Classification: LCC JA85.P678 2018 | DDC 320.01/4--dc23

Manufactured in the United States of America

Website: http://greenhavenpublishing.com

Contents

Introduction

As might be expected from a book entitled *Populism in the Digital Age*, the articles compiled herein examine the interaction between two separate but closely related phenomena: today's increasingly networked online public sphere, and the populist political movements of both the past and present. Have digital media ushered in a new era of direct participation in politics globally? Or is social media's promise of a "megaphone for all" undermining the democratic process? Does the internet facilitate new social alignments, or does it merely provide an outlet for trolls to articulate offensive views without fear of repercussions? Are perennial social conflicts between rich and poor, insiders and outsiders, men and women, and people of color and whites getting worse? These tensions have simmered for centuries with no sign of abatement, but the connective technology enabling our digital public sphere has arguably created a situation of extreme and perhaps unbridgeable polarization. If it has, we must now reckon with an entirely novel state of political affairs that is threatening to further unravel.

Social theorists call the fundamental alteration of our knowledge and assumptions and the outcomes they produce a "paradigm shift." Several viewpoints in this resource identify digital populism as an example of this type of shift and foreground the internet's tremendous impact on both the democratic process and public discourse. The extent to which this shift has been beneficial or purely disruptive is an open question and one on which many experts disagree. To some, the rapid, seemingly haphazard way some issues gain traction while others fade into obscurity is chaotic, distracting, and ultimately negative. More sanguine authors point to the liberating potential of decentered information flows and increased social connectivity. While much has been made of the internet as a vast "echo chamber" in which one individually curates one's worldview, we will read at least one viewpoint that is skeptical as to whether sites like Facebook and Twitter truly create "bubbles" any more than a steady and exclusive diet of Fox News or the *Nation* would in a traditional media landscape. The more historically minded authors cast recent and noteworthy populist outcries such as Donald Trump's victory or Brexit as simply the latest manifestations of age-old resentments inherent to representative democracy and capitalist inequality.

Distrust of elected officials, anti-elitism, xenophobia, nationalism, and a general mood of anti-politics are all symptomatic of populism in the digital age. It is therefore worthwhile to step back and look at American populism in its original context of the late nineteenth century to see how it differed from its current iteration. In the 1880s and 1890s, the United States economy became highly centralized and also marked by great inequalities in income and wealth. Throughout the nation, Wall Street financiers and industrial tycoons held outsized power. In the rural South, sharecroppers and tenant farmers found their interests pitted against that of the planter class, represented politically by the powerful Bourbon Democrats. As the price of crops fell and the United States entered a bitter depression, many of these farmers found it difficult to survive. Rather than dispute each other on minute differences, they made common cause against their common class enemies and began to organize. What began as a loose affiliation between the Southern Farmers' Alliance and the Colored Farmers' Alliance evolved into the official Populist Party, which was founded in St. Louis in 1892.

While it is unlikely that the Populist Party was completely free of racism, early Populist leaders understood that the wealthy exploited racial animosity to weaken the bonds of potential shared class interests across racial lines and fought against such tactics. Moreover, women were instrumental to campaign activities, and an important part of the Populist platform was the establishment of women's colleges throughout the South for career training. Other signature issues of the Populist Party included support for unions and organized labor, a progressive income tax, and government control of utilities. The Populists won 8.5 percent of the popular presidential vote and made impressive gains in state legislatures. It would not last. Mainstream Democrats used intimidation, fraud, propaganda, and co-optation to crush the Populist Party's electoral hopes, as well as the broader goals of the movement.

Independent Vermont senator and former presidential candidate Bernie Sanders is perhaps the closest contemporary ideological heir of the original populist position. Seizing on the political momentum of the Occupy movement and tapping into a mood of anger and frustration with business as usual, Sanders brought income inequality, the fight for a living wage, universal access to education, a single payer health care system, and progressive taxation back into mainstream political discussion. And similar to his nineteenth century forebears, Sanders's electoral hopes were actively sabotaged by the Democratic Party's wealthy donor class and "business friendly" stance. Moreover, Sanders did not fare as well as the early populists in fostering class unity across the racial divide.

The Black Lives Matter movement began as a spontaneous online response to the extrajudicial killing of black people by police. What began as a hashtag soon had over fifty chapters nationwide, as well as a comprehensive vision to identify and ameliorate the many threats and systemic injustices people of color face daily. Despite Sanders's status as a natural ally to the movement, some vocal Black Lives Matter activists were disappointed by what they saw as his subordination of racial concerns to economic matters. Black people were being shot with impunity by cops, while the school to prison pipeline insured highly disproportionate imprisonment of black men. Surely a more subtle response was needed, or so reasoned the Black Lives Matter activists. Although Sanders integrated the group's concerns into his platform, his campaign was never as effective in mobilizing people of color as it was in creating the now infamous and almost exclusively white "Bernie bros."

Of course, Donald Trump's rise and shocking presidential victory is a version of populism unique to the digital stage. A wealthy real estate developer, Manhattan socialite, and television personality is perhaps a most unlikely populist. Trump's lack of a fixed position on any issue allowed him to say whatever it took to gain attention and popularity. Though not aligned ideologically with the traditional concerns of economic populism, Trump's lack of political experience, anti-immigrant sentiments, and nationalist credo to "make America great again" echoed some of the baser tactics of historical populists. Though accusations that the Trump campaign colluded with Russian operatives and fake news "bots" have yet to yield a smoking gun, the Trump campaign unquestionably recognized the value of social media advertising dollars in reaching undecided voters. Donald Trump's lack of experience, temperamental unfitness for office, and disdain for poor "losers" illustrates how the digital age has distorted populism. Indeed, it is unlikely Trump's policies and positions, if he can be said to possess any, will aid the common working person.

Populism began as a coherent set of principles to redress poverty and inequality. It is now something else entirely, though some overlap remains identifiable to the keen historical observer. The nature of this evolution, and the role technology and new media have played in it, are the twin questions explored in *At Issue: Populism in the Digital Age.* An aim of this book is to unify disparate perspectives and enable a new generation of keen historians to base their conclusions on solid ground.

1

The Origin of Populism

Nancy MacLean

Nancy MacLean is an American historian and the William H. Chafe Professor of History and Public Policy at Duke University. She is also the author of several books, including Democracy in Chains: The Deep History of the Radical Right's Stealth Plan for America.

In this opening viewpoint, Nancy MacLean traces the roots of the populist movement back to the late nineteenth century. At this time, the United States was suffering a deep depression. Prices for crops such as cotton fell to unprofitable levels. Under the leadership of Tom Watson, the radical southern arm of the newly formed Populist Party unified struggling black and white voters along class lines. Among other reforms, its platform included support for labor unions and a graduated income tax. Despite electoral victories, the movement was crushed by fraud and intimidation, as well as co-optation and false promises from mainstream Democrats.

I t was an event without precedent in the South. On a few day's notice, 2,000 white farmers dropped their work, picked up their guns and rode in from across the state to Thomson, Ga. They came to defend a young Black preacher threatened with lynching for his political activities.

The year was 1892, an election year. The Black man, H.S. Doyle, was under attack by the Southern ruling class for having made

"The Promise and Failure of Populism," by Nancy MacLean, International Socialist Organization, April 27, 2012. Reprinted by permission.

63 speeches in support of Tom Watson, the white congressional candidate of the newly formed People's (Populist) Party, and the main leader of the southern and most radical wing of that party.

Populism emerged in response to the frightful conditions faced by small farmers, tenants and sharecroppers in the 1880s and 1890s. In these years, steadily growing numbers of them became dependent on the "crop-lien system" for credit—a system that turned them into virtual debt slaves and forced them to plant more and more of their land in cotton.

Yet the price of cotton continued to fall, from a dollar a pound at the end of the Civil War to 7 cents a pound in 1891—less than it cost to produce. To these already poor farmers, the depression of the 1890s—the worst in American history until the 1930s—was the last straw. For many, their survival was at stake.

All this had taken place under the reign of the "Bourbon Democrats," an alliance of planters and new industrialists who ruled the South unchallenged since the defeat of Reconstruction in the 1870s. These Democrats had relied upon racism to keep themselves in power, using the specter of "Black rule" to keep poor whites in line.

But faced with the crisis conditions of the 1880s and 1890s, many Southern farmers, Black and white, began to think for themselves. They realized that their only hope lay in united struggle against the big planters and capitalists.

In the late 1880s, they began to organize cooperative efforts to deal with their problems. By 1890, some 3 million white farmers belonged to the Southern Farmers' Alliance, and 1.25 million southern Black farmers belonged to the Colored Farmers' National Alliance. These groups, along with fledgling unions in urban areas, provided the basis for the Populist Party, founded in St. Louis in 1892.

Denouncing both major parties as "tools of the capitalists," the Populists adopted a broad platform. It included: changes in the currency system that would help debt-stricken farmers and workers; support for organized labor and for a shorter workday for industrial workers; government ownership of public utilities; a graduated income tax; and many democratic reforms of the nation's political system, such as the right to referendums, recall and female suffrage.

Millions of farmers and workers found in the Populist program a voice for their anger at the gross inequalities and injustices of American society at the time.

In 1892, the Populist presidential candidate won over a million votes—8.5 percent of the total electorate—and over 1,500 Populist candidates won election to state legislatures.

Clearly, the Populists were a force to be reckoned with. Yet their greatest threat was not in the specific reforms they called for, but rather in the future they looked to. In the South, the Populists threatened the mainstay of ruling class power: division among the exploited. As Tom Watson explained to Black and white farmers:

> You are kept apart that you may be fleeced separately of your earnings. You are made to hate each other because upon that hatred rests the financial despotism that enslaves you both. You are deceived and blinded that you may not see how this race antagonism perpetuates a system that beggars both.

The Populists were not explicitly anti-racist, but they emphatically defended political rights and equality for Blacks and insisted on the common economic interests of the oppressed and exploited. As Watson said, "The accident of color can make no difference in the interests of farmers, croppers and laborers."

For the South—indeed, for the entire U.S. at that time—this was a revolutionary stand. Its result was to briefly bring Blacks and whites together in a common class struggle the likes of which had never been seen before or since in the South.

The response of the Southern ruling class was swift and effective. Through fraud, bribery, intimidation, violence and terror, they denied Populists their rights and stole their hard-won electoral victories. In 1892 alone, 155 Blacks and 100 whites died at the hands of lynchers. Throughout the South, armed planters hauled their Black sharecroppers to the polls in wagonloads and forced them to vote for the Democratic Party.

But brutality and fraud were not the only tools in the chest of the ruling class. Another was to rekindle irrational white fears of Blacks through vicious racist propaganda.

And then there was co-optation. The Democratic Party did an about-face in 1896, putting forth a presidential candidate who spouted the rhetoric of reform in order to steal the Populists' thunder. The Democrats had no intention of making any real changes, but the more far-sighted realized that they had to pay lip service to reform in order to contain the spread of radicalism.

Through such tactics, the Democrats managed to defeat the Populist movement and defuse its threat to ruling class power.

The movement had its own internal problems that contributed to defeat, of course. It was neither a working class–based nor socialist movement, and as such, it had no chance of fundamentally changing the capitalist society in which it grew. Likewise, class conflicts existed even within the movement, between medium-sized planters like Watson, and the Black and white tenants they employed.

But even with its limitations, the Populist movement gives us an inspiring glimpse of what a united struggle by the exploited can achieve, and of how quickly old prejudices and fears can change in a common fight around common interests. No other movement of the time held such promise for the rural poor.

Its defeat, therefore, ushered in an era of disaster for the 90 percent of Black Americans who still lived on the land, and for their one-time allies among poor whites.

The defeat of Populism led to unprecedented reaction and repression. Beginning with Mississippi in 1890, the ruling Democrats devised a series of limits on voting rights that effectively disenfranchised Blacks—and later many poor whites—throughout the South. At the same time, they wrote the practice of segregation into Jim Crow laws.

The disillusionment and bitterness bred by defeat made poor whites vulnerable to the worst sort of demagoguery. Democratic Party politicians made the manipulation of racism their stock in trade, using it to distract poor whites from their real problems and their real enemies, while their own conditions grew worse by the year. Many former populists, including Tom Watson, became virulent racists.

The demise of the Populist movement was thus a defeat for almost all concerned. All, that is, except the ruling class that organized this defeat, and the Democratic Party, which stole only enough of the Populists' platform to derail the movement.

Once again, the Democratic Party earned its reputation as the graveyard of American radicalism.

2

Left and Right Wing Populism

Thomas DeMichele

Thomas DeMichele is the head author and content strategist for websites like FactMyth.com, CryptoCurrencyFacts.com, and ObamaCareFacts.com.

In the following viewpoint, Thomas DeMichele explores the similarities and crucial differences between populist movements on the left and right wings of the political spectrum. Both movements articulate frustration with capitalist-driven inequality, and both are also anti-elitist movements that are prone to authoritarianism. However, left-wing populism is socially liberal and seeks global equality. On the other hand, right-wing populism is typically conservative on social issues and favors exclusionary tactics, xenophobia, and racism. When right-wing populism is tethered to authoritarian power, fascism becomes a danger. On the other hand, left-wing populism risks giving the state too much power.

The Difference Between the Two Main Types of Populism; Or, National "Right-Wing" Populism and Socially Progressive "Left-Wing" Populism Are Different

Right-wing Populism, like the Tea Party, and Left-wing Populism, like Bernie Sanders, are the two basic forms of populism. Both are anti-elite but otherwise very different. The main notable difference

"'Right-Wing' Populism and 'Left-Wing' Populism Are Different," by Thomas DeMichele, FactMyth, April 6, 2017. Reprinted by permission.

being that one is left-wing and one is right-wing in terms of social issues.[1,2,3,4,5]

With the above in mind, the Tea Party and Senator Sanders are each only emblematic of complex movements that have their roots in much of our shared western history (so try not to get sidetracked by specific figures and movements used as examples).

The reality is populists come in all flavors, for every voter issue, there is a populist and elite faction. Sometimes populists team up over an issue, sometimes two factions of populists are bitter enemies. It really all depends on what issues are driving the populist sentiment!

Below we will discuss modern right-wing and left-wing populism in its many forms (including both passive and authoritative forms and organized and disorganized forms) from Communism and Fascism to "the modern global alt-left and alt-right" (for lack of a better term).

This will show us how a "spray tan fascist" like Le Pen, is different from a Confederate, is different from anti-fa, is different from William Jennings Bryan, is different from a Know-Nothing, is Different from a Bolshevik, etc.

With that said, one should note that we can trace the roots of left-right populism back as far back as we can trace oppression and classism. We can trace it back to the Populist Party, Know-Nothings, Cromwell's Army, Confederates, Communards, Jacobins, the Shirtless Spanish, Spartacus' slave rebellion, Caesar's Plebeian Revolution, etc, etc.

If the elite are oppressing the plebs, in any era, which is most eras, a populist reaction is ensured (excepted in the most despotic of states).

It is more a natural human response to the effects of inequality (and otherwise just the sentiment of "the many"… even when that "many" is actually "minority interest" that calls itself "a majority party") rearing its head again and again throughout history, than it is something new.

In this way populism is like a canary in a coal mine, if you start seeing pitchforks, you should look closely at what policies are creating the social, political, and economic gap that is driving the frustration and do your best to stop the next Caesar before they crown themselves God-King; unless you are more a Caesar type than a Cicero type, and I mean people are, the World Wars didn't start themselves you know.

TIP: The vast accumulation of capital and the ensuing corruption of the Senate and Oligarchs in the most liberal of times (see Athens, Rome, and essentially the entire globe in modern times) is all fun and games, until the bottom part of the pyramid gets frenzied and is led by a serpent with a golden tongue who becomes the champion of the people before becoming a tyrant. There are many books that explain this, I suggest Plato's (as it offers not only an examination of a problem, but common sense solutions known since at least 380 BC).

[…]

The Difference Between Right-Wing and Left-Wing Populism

Before we can understand how the left-wing and right-wing version of populism are different, we have to understand how they are the same:

- Right-wing populism and left-wing populism are both sentiments of frustration felt by the working class that arise as political movements.
- Both Right-wing populism and left-wing populism can be said to be "anti-elite" or "anti-establishment" generally speaking. We can say they are, in Marxian terms, "the anti-bourgeoisie proletariat" of the left and right. That is less a judgement call, and more the language used to describe these movements back between the mid 1800's up to WWII.
- They are both collectivist to some extent.
- They can both be authoritative or not. That is important and we discuss it below.

- They both want "progressive" revolutionary change, typically by democratic means, but not always.
- They both are responses to political, social, and economic inequality (the inequality may spring from global neoliberalism or oppressive national policy, in this cycle, it is from global neoliberalism which is cultural, political, and economic globalism in the liberal democratic state, including, of course, immigration policy and social welfare; but that changes in different eras).

Those common factors aside, the two types of populism are opposites on social issues with polar opposite statist solutions, where:

- **Right-wing populism favors small groups and inequality** (which can manifest as protectionism, nativism, nationalism, and xenophobia; which can look like activist social conservatism or even fascism).
- **Left-wing populism favors equality and big groups** (which can manifest as socially minded globalization and a socially minded welfare state; which can look like progressive social liberalism, social democracy, or even socialism).

In other words, while they are both anti-elitist collectivist movements, the key difference is one is socially conservative and focused on a small group and the other socially liberal and favors global social equality.

With that in mind, Right-wing populism and left-wing populism can be further differentiated and described in this way (keeping in mind any specific movement of the populist left or right will have its own planks):

- **Modern Right-Wing Populism In Action**: It is a socially conservative anti-elitist sentiment that believes in the social hierarchy. Like the ENF, The Tea Party, Alt-Right, States' Rights South, and at an extreme WWII Fascist Populism. It is anti-global-elite, protectionist, nationalist, and often militant. The Highest Good is "the State" classically speaking, but more broadly in modern terms "the in-group." So in the modern west right-wing populism tends to arise as sentiment against "others" AKA intolerance (for example intolerant of "Illegals", Liberals, Feminists, Progressives, different faiths and races, etc.). Generally, a radical socially conservative exclusive fascist movement that demands radical action against others, conformity, aggression, and identity politics. We might call this **National Populism (AKA Populist Nationalism) or Right-Wing Populism**.

- **Modern Left-Wing Populism in Action**: It is a socially liberal progressive anti-elitist sentiment that believes in class equality and in some instances even nationlessness and classlessness. Like Progressivism, Socialism, and at an extreme WWII Communist populism. It is a pro-worker, pro-globalist, internationalist, and "green" movement that supports the welfare state (social safety net and social equality). The Highest Good is Social Equality for the have-nots. In practice, it can be anti-classical liberal, anti-socially conservative, and nationalist (like how Bernie wants jobs at home AND "fair-trade"). Although, in some cases, it can be militant with groups like Leninists and anti-Fas, in the modern West it tends to be more passive and less organized than its right-wing neighbor. We might call this **Socially Liberal "Progressive" Populism or Left-Wing Populism**. TIP: Modern left-wing populism is often notably less militaristic, aggressive, and intolerant than the right-wing form (it can be radical and PC, but generally is less aggressive and organized, with anti-fa being the exception to this rule), this isn't the case in every era (consider the October Revolution for example), but it is today… and that means were aren't purely discussing equal opposites here in 2017 in the West. With that noted, outside of the west, if we consider statist socialism like we find in Venezuela or North Korea, then obviously the tendency is toward control and militarism and away from populist sentiment.

TIP: Both Anonymous and ISIS can be thought of as populist groups. Anonymous is a non-political group that can be described as disorganized non-authoritative left-wing populist collective, and ISIS is an organized right-wing populist authoritative collective that is in many ways fascist. One may also have a populist movement of another form, such as a libertarian populist movement, but here we want to examine the general left and right forms of populism before jumping into other complexities. As you hopefully can tell already, both types of populism have their pros and cons, and each speak to the more general left-right political split.

TIP: Notice how both groups are a bit collectivist and nationalist (both turning to the state for solutions)? The left-wing is more collectivist and inclusive, and the right-wing one more nationalist and exclusive, but they have common elements. That sort of near commonality can be confusing, but these two populist movements are as different as Fascism and Communism because they are the roots of those WWII extremes.

TIP: I have a theory that these sentiments and movements are naturally occurring (where for example the natural desire for equality arises as the left-wing type). I think it helps explain the two identities (and why they keep reappearing in the mid-1800's, in the 1910's, in the 1940's, in the 1960's, today), but don't want to get sidetracked by it here (but do read it).

TIP: Both types are seeking policies that help their group, the left-wing type by its nature favors a bigger group and thus can look more attractive on paper, but each type has vices and virtues.

NOTES: See a basic left-right spectrum for a deeper understanding of what creates what we call "left-wing" and "right-wing." One should consider populism, like any other political attribute, both broadly and per-issue. A libertarian form of populism might be called left-right populism, and it would be a non-authoritative economic form of populism. Further such distinctions can be made by understanding the core attributes related to left-right and political ideologies in action.

Populism also Comes in Authoritarian and Non-Authoritarian Forms and Organized and Disorganized Forms

It is vital to note that either type of populism can be authoritative or not per-issue and can be organized or not.

When either left or the right type of populism becomes authoritative, and especially when it is organized, and thus forces these policies on the other wings and center with the might of many in coordinated lock-step, it becomes (often in practice) despotic and tyrannical (and therefore not republican, democratic, or liberal).

When it does not force itself, and/or is disorganized, when it is passive, it avoids many of the offenses and may even be thought of as a tolerable balancing force.

Both the core left and right types are going to put workers' first and take care of their own, and both have their virtues and vices (some more virtuous in a given cycle, but both have their vices).

The major problem with populism isn't that it exists, or even that it has a seat at the table. It is like the old beast with many heads, the tyrannical mob. All the populist rage can disrupt the centered democracy that everyone else is busy working with, especially in times of economic hardship where people look to radical solutions.

[...]

The Problems With Populism—The Vices of Excess and Deficiency

The virtues of the types of populism are not the problem. When the types remain in their balanced and non-extreme forms, they each have a number of respectable qualities. For example, their focus on the have-not working class is admirable, and so is their focus on taking care of "their own." No one faults parents for putting their children first. It isn't these qualities in which their problems reside; it is in these qualities unrestrained and in extremes.

The Problem With Right-Wing Populism

The problem with the right-wing version of populism specifically is "their own" likely doesn't include you.

This is arguably OK when the populism isn't authoritative (such as with a non-violent racial separatist). However, when it becomes authoritative, it can look like Nazi Germany or the Deep South during Reconstruction.

In fact, it may just *Ban* you, or use the state to stop your *Sessions*.

Civil liberties and rights are cast aside for the wants of a small group to make X region great again for a particular group of people. This is a fear-based economy of tyranny and despotism rooted in xenophobia and in-group nativist nationalism, specifically the fascist kind (by common definition).

TIP: [...] Right-wing populism isn't new; instead, it is essentially fascism re-branded. It has been called New Populism in the past. Each iteration has a unique ideology and strategy, but it's like the difference between Maoism and Stalinism (not much consolation to the other wing; still no).

The Problem With Left-Wing Populism

The problem with left-wing populism is that trying to make everyone equal and submitting authority to a "strong man" of the state to get this done is a slippery slope in a few directions.

Like the right-wing version, if the left-wing populists stay in their sphere and don't act authoritatively, it is tolerable.

However, when the left-wing populists start using a big stick like the guillotine happy Jacobins, Stalin's Militant Communists, or the puritanical Prohibitionists, then this too becomes just as tyrannical and despotic as the most extreme form of fascism.

This type is to the left of the right-wing type, as it favors a bigger group, but that aside, they are both "to the right" of classical liberalism in terms of authority.

TIP: Just like not all right-wing populism is "exactly the same," neither are all types of socialism. There are both populist and authoritarian types; some want a planned economy, some just generally support a safety net. See the many types of socialism.

Conclusions to the Problems in General and Other Nuances

This is to say, the problem with both types of populism, be they socially liberal moralists or socially conservative nationalist nativists, is that both types of populists want to do something "extreme," and extremes corrupt democracy.

Namely, they want to destroy the upper-class bourgeoisie capitalists (AKA "The Establishment") who own the means of production and control labor and form a new government based on their ideals.

When people get enough power and exert enough authority, it can get messy.

TIP: Here we can get into the ills of the extreme authoritarianism it takes to make radical change, and the problems of extreme liberalism some non-authoritarian populist types want, but that is a conversation we can resume later. One can be populist Green, Libertarian, Constitutionalist, Maoist, Tory, Labour, Anarchist, etc. We can exhaust a list of every issue and ideology that can contain an elite and populist wing, but I don't want to get too far into that conversation here. We aren't making judgment calls on underlying policy stances here, but rather just differentiating between general left and right types of populism to show their basic vices and virtues. We also have non-authoritative versions that have their own ills of excess and deficiency (such as a pure libertarian state without rules which can be said to be populist in nature). This line of thinking is noted here, but you can see the basics of populism for more discussion on that.

How to Help Ensure Populist Sentiment Stays Productive and Not Tyrannical in a Democratically Minded Republic

None of the above should be considered to be slander against a Sanders, Sessions, or Bannon, or against a specific ideology, or against the left or right, or against a form of government.

In fact, I like William Jennings Bryan and Bernie Sanders, and I assume some on the right like Calhoun and Steve Bannon. Others might like Mises. Nothing is wrong with any of that philosophically.

Likewise, I love Representative Democracy, and I'm sure others prefer a more ordered or less ordered state.

We can have equality, have our liberty, and we can put our country first. We have a mixed government meant to facilitate such things. We just don't want any of this in extremes that *alienate* our other factions in a democratic state. There are few greater ironies than an alienated faction becoming alienators themselves after rising to power.

We can have our cake and eat it too, but if we ration the cake by putting people in death camps or by forcing them into social systems they don't want to be in, then well yes that is philosophically on paper and in action problematic.

Certainly, there is nothing wrong with feeling frustration toward the elite in an environment of political, social, and economic inequality, since when have elites been saints? I don't recall a point in history, and certainly not today.

There is something wrong. Actually, there are some big problems with the anarchistic Jacobin revolution that many suffering from political, economic, or social inequality seem to want so badly.

What is wrong is that it flies in the face of all of political history and our Constitution.

While the elite classes, globally and locally, can be seen as corrupt (we've all be frustrated by their oligarchical aspects, both on the populist left and right), that doesn't mean the answer lays in extremes.

Extreme equality and extreme liberty corrupt democracy, deficiencies of liberty and equality corrupt democracy, democracy corrupts oligarchy, oligarchy corrupts timocracy, timocracy corrupts aristocracy, and aristocracies are often corrupt.

But Madison knew that; Jefferson knew that; Washington knew that, Adams, Henry, etc.

Why did they know it? They knew it because they read Plato and Montesquieu, because they read both Hobbes and Locke, because they read Machiavelli and Buchanan.

They looked to Athens, Sparta, Rome, the Italian Republics, France, Scotland, and England and they said, "well, we want better for all, not just better for some."

They took the principles of republicanism seriously; they used reason, they respected law and order. They didn't just use the principles as talking points to strip rights from their opposition like witch hunting puritans.

That is why they created a Mixed-Republic, to safeguard against tyranny and meant to temper the different naturally occurring factions that arise.

Not just temper the left and right, but temper the authoritarian with the liberal, the elite with the populist, the fascist with the communist when things got too extreme, equality and inequality, liberty and illiberally.

It is a statement of balancing virtues, in the holiest of western traditions. It is the "Civil Religion" of the United States (which includes our actual religion; i.e. this isn't a statement on a state without faith).

In other words, the difference between the two forms of populism is as clear as the difference between Bernie Sanders and Steve Bannon. Or, in WWII, when speaking of the authoritarian versions, the difference between Stalin and Hitler.

The problem with both forms of populism is that their vendetta against the elites is similar to the left going to war with the right or like the foot going to war against the mouth, uncomfortable, absurd, and not very useful.

You can't go to war with a naturally occurring social system. Only a eugenicist or tyrant goes to war against their children. Are we Saturn or Athena here? Alex Jones howls about eugenics, but if he pushes us off a populist cliff, what exactly does he think is going to happen? How exactly does Marx's revolution destroy a naturally occurring system? It doesn't.

Marx was wrong generally speaking (in his call for revolution and Communist economics, not in his account of history or his general theory of economics), I thought we agreed? How come we agree on his economic system being wrong, but yet we have the right-wing populists trying to implement his revolution. *That* is absurd, *that* is alienating, *that* is… pretty nuts from a historic perspective no matter what your ends.

Still, rants aside, and to the point, populism isn't a fad that can be stamped out, and neither is elitism. Both are responses to imbalances of the virtues of the state.

Factions aren't supposed to like each other, they are supposed to temper each other, that is why we have a mixed Republic.

This is to say, they are different in just about every way, but they are the same in being emblematic of responses to political and economic inequality (AKA the secret sauce of Marx's revolution in action).

It may be too late for the neoliberals and neocons to reign things back in even if they wanted to; or it may not.

How does one cure extreme inequality without turning too much toward the welfare state when political parties are divided, factions rabid, and people already feeling the effects of political, economic, and social inequality?

I'm not sure beyond looking to the original spirit and letter of the law and our founding philosophers and history. Even when we know, we still have to act. And I mean, look Steve Bannon and Bernie aren't wrong for placing their frustrations with the elite, it is just we all seem to be on a global slippery slope that mirrors WWII.

Perhaps the realization that populist vs. elite is just like left vs. right, democrat vs. republican, communist vs. fascist, a natural response to life complexities (all capable of being extreme when the scales become unbalanced) will help.

At the very least, we have a reminder not to confuse socially liberal populists with right-wing national nativist populists; they share essentially no commonalities except being "anti-elite" although they don't seem to agree on which elite they are anti.

Also, to all the right-wing populists out there, you have to remember which teams were Axis and which teams were Allies in WWII. I'm not snarky, as WWII was one of the worst events in human history and the idea is to avoid any like battles of global left-right factions. However, if a big group fights a small group, who do you think is going to win? Well, we never know. But I'll tell you, most Americans and Westerners are going to be fighting for liberalism and not against it.

Right now that fight is happening democratically (free speech, votes, etc.) and within the bounds of general reason and law. History is clear. World Wars are catastrophic.

We should have more respect for history, or we will be doomed to repeat it. We have to agree on a democratic center, and we can start dipping our toes in far-left or far-right water, even when it is tempting. Not because some don't like it, but because we have to tend to the wants and needs of the whole diverse group.

Conclusion

In basic terms every ideology that is political comes in a left-wing and right-wing form, it is no surprise that it is the same for populism.

Really we are just saying "the left-wing and right-wing of the anti-elite working class that arise in response to inequality in the liberal state"… although when we phrase it that way we realize "uh, oh, that is totally what happened in WWII".

And yes, of course, and this is the problem.

We haven't "gone there" yet as a nation/globe, but the World Wide fad represented by the ENF is a real cause for concern, and since it is, we should also not ignore the other four obvious place to look "the populist left" and establishment right and left.

The answer has never been in extremes and has always been in centered positions (which also have a left and right), one would the answer to be no different here. We need to bring justified beliefs to the center and has this out before it goes too far.

Citations

1. Right-wing populism, https://en.wikipedia.org/wiki/Right-wing_populism

2. Left-wing populism, https://en.wikipedia.org/wiki/Left-wing_populism

3. How Steve Bannon helped bring a nationalist, populist agenda to the White House, http://www.pbs.org/newshour/bb/steve-bannon-helped-bring-nationalist-populist-agenda-white-house/

4. No easy answers: why left-wing economics is not the answer to right-wing populism, https://www.vox.com/world/2017/3/13/14698812/bernie-trump-corbyn-left-wing-populism

5. Tony Blair: Against Populism, the Center Must Hold, https://www.nytimes.com/2017/03/03/opinion/tony-blair-against-populism-the-center-must-hold.html?_r=0

3

Understanding the Black Lives Matter Movement

Iris Wijers

Iris Wijers is a student of communication sciences whose research interests include big data, data analysis, politics, social media, and viral marketing. She is a writer for Diggit Magazine, *an academic news and information platform.*

In the following viewpoint, Iris Wijers analyzes the Black Lives Matter movement. Black Lives Matter emerged from a spontaneous eruption of anger and frustration following the acquittal of George Zimmerman, the neighborhood watch vigilante who fatally shot Trayvon Martin. Drawing on the power of new media to galvanize shared sentiments, Black Lives Matter began as a Twitter hashtag in 2013 but has since morphed into a vital political force impacting life both online and off, with over thirty chapters spread across the United States. Its message overlaps with the civil rights movement but also seeks to elevate the voices and perspectives of women and other marginalized groups within the black community.

W hat started out as a public outcry in 2013, following the acquittal of the police officer who shot Trayvon Martin, has since then morphed into a full-blown social movement. This paper analyses the formation and enduring existence of the Black Lives Matter movement through new media.

About This Analysis

This analysis of the Black Lives Matter movement (hereafter: BLM) attempts to illustrate how a hashtag, set up by three women, could mobilize the outrage of an oppressed group of people across the US. Special attention will be paid to how a movement that found its origins online, can strongly impact the offline world. I will also emphasize that the movement has flourished in the way that it has, because of the influence of new types of media formats that are available nowadays. The mobilizing ability of the BLM movement is analyzed using the concepts of networked social movements (Castells, 2013), addressivity (Bakhtin, 1984; as quoted by Maly, 2014) and choreography of assembly (Gerbaudo, 2012). Furthermore, the discussion about the identity of the BLM movement is also addressed within the framework of discursive battle (Maly, 2014; Maly, 2016), ideology (Blommaert, 2005) and message (Lempert and Silverstein, 2012).

Messages in the media from and about the BLM movement were analyzed and in order to evaluate the self-presentation of the movement, social media channels, like Twitter and Facebook, were included in the analysis. The Black Lives Matter website was used as an important source to determine the self-presentation and message of the BLM movement. In order to contextualize the movement, media and their presentation of the movement, both supportive and critical, were also analyzed. Content from 2013 to January 2017 was used in this analysis, but special attention was given to more recent content.

An Introduction: #Blacklivesmatter

The Black Lives Matter movement will not have escaped the attention of those of us who have been observant of the American political system. Since 2013 the movement has grown rapidly, advocating the rights of black Americans both offline and online. The BLM movement epitomizes the power of new media to mobilize public outrage into a movement.

The movement started in 2013 as a hashtag (#BlackLivesMatter) on Twitter. The hashtag was first set up by Patrisse Cullors in response to outrage amongst the black community after George Zimmerman was acquitted for the shooting of young African-American Trayvon Martin. Cullors shared a Facebook post of grief and condolences by Alicia Garza, first using the hashtag to give a voice to the words of both love and outrage. Alica Garza, Opal Tometi and Patrisse Cullors subsequently decided to give a voice to the outraged community of African-Americans, by setting up social media accounts for the movement and by making their movement a presence in the offline community as well, by organising a march and making signs (Day, 2015). As more shootings followed, the movement grew, moving from an online outcry to a movement that was also firmly present in the streets: after Ferguson, people rioted and a "freedom ride" was organized. After Charleston, supporters of Black Lives Matter occupied a shopping mall and later the phrase 'Black lives matter' was merchandised and adopted by politicians (Day, 2015).

There are over 30 chapters of BLM across the US at the moment and the Black Lives Matter movement has become a household name in political debates. The BLM movement has a website where it chronicles its own origins and discusses what the movement stands for. What started out as simply a hashtag has become a more 'official' movement with the addition of this website and the creation of chapters across the US. This website also allowed the BLM movement to create a more coherent ideology for supporters to act in accordance with and turned the movement from a hasthag into a real, tangible, social movement that could use political and social pressure to advocate for black people's rights. I will discuss the message and ideology of the BLM movement in the following section.

BLM, Message & Ideology

Message

Lempert and Silverstein (2012) originally use the concept of 'message' when discussing politicians. I have repurposed this idea to talk about the Black Lives Matter movement as a whole, which can be seen as a 'political actor' in its own right. A message, in political parlance, is the portrayed character of a political entity. It is crafted from various elements like a biography: issues that the entity is involved with and its style (Lempert & Silverstein, 2012).

The message of the BLM movement is presented clearly on the website of the movement. An important part of message are the issues someone is concerned with. The issues that the BLM movement is involved with seem straightforward: the lives of black people, and specifically the fight for equality. The link with the Civil Rights Movement is one that is quickly drawn and one that is drawn by the movement itself as well. A banner prominently featured on the 'who we are' page of the BLM website quotes civil rights activist Diane Nash. By quoting an activist from the Civil Rights Movement, the BLM movement shows affiliation with this movement and their ideology, already sending the message that their ideals are similar and that they are speaking from within a tradition of black struggle and black empowerment.

Furthermore, while the issue of police brutality has become somewhat ingrained in the BLM movement, the movement itself clearly states that it's concerned with a much wider range of issues, also regarding oppression and marginalization within the black community. On their 'guiding principles' page the movement noticably states that *ALL* black lives matter, referring especially to transgender and queer members of the black community (Black Lives matter, n.d.). On the website, the following statement can be found: "*Black Lives Matter is a unique contribution that goes beyond extrajudicial killings of Black people by police and vigilantes. It goes beyond the narrow nationalism that can be prevalent within Black communities, which merely call on Black people to love Black, live*

33

Black and buy Black, keeping straight cis Black men in the front of the movement while our sisters, queer and trans and disabled folk take up roles in the background or not at all." (Black Lives Matter, n.d.).

The quote is telling for what the Black Lives Matter movement aspires to be. On the one hand they quote the Civil Rights Movement and identify with it, but they criticise it as well. At it's core, the Black Lives Matter can be seen as a feministic and LGBTQ-friendly version of the Civil Rights Movement. It will come as no surprise then that the civil rights activist the movement quotes, is female. In line with this, the BLM 'origin story' is called a 'herstory' by the movement, a term mostly associated with feminism. The quoted text speaks out against the history of black heterosexual, cisgendered men taking credit for the work of black, queer, women. The Black Lives Matter movement calls out the black community itself on its treatment of minorities within the community.

While the BLM movement is thus generally associated with police violence and the fight against racism, the BLM movement is also partially a feminist movement for LGBTQ people. In the words of the movement: *"To the Black mothers, elders, trans women, queer sisters, femmes, young women and girls and comrades on the frontlines that refuse to let police, politicians, provocateurs, or patriarchy destroy our collective will to get free. We see you."* (Black Lives Matter, n.d.) The quote clearly states the support for minorities within the black community that BLM stands for and clearly incites a fight against the patriarcy. Somewhat ironically, this message doesn't seem to have resonated in the way that the outrage against police violence has, showing that the BLM still has more than one fight to win.

Ideology, Hegemony and Discourse
Using the parts of the message described above, the ideology that the BLM movement promotes can be distilled. An ideology is a perspective on the world, shared by a group of actors. It is often associated with a certain set of symbolic representations, such as discourses, images and stereotypes, as well as with certain

behaviours and ideals (Blommaert, 2005). The ideology of the BLM movement is to create a society where black people are no longer marginalized and wherein racism is truly a thing of the past. Emphasis is placed on the fact that *all* black lives matter equally, and the ideology of the BLM movement includes a strong disapproval of heteronormativity and the patriarchy, somewhat putting it at odds with people within the black community as well. It would be amiss not to mention the strong influence of feminism and feminist ideology on the ideology that permeates the BLM movement. The BLM movement can therefore be thought of as combating more than one hegemony.

Hegemony is the coming together of power and ideology (Blommaert, 2005). It is a relevant term with which to discuss the fight of the BLM movement. Blommaert (2005) argues that many contemporary anti-racism movements are not anti-hegemonic, because they do not challenge the systemic forms of racism, but simply address the way people act in society. While the idea that black and white people are equal and that society should treat them equally isn't shocking anymore to most people, it is clear that the BLM movement is anti-hegemonic in suggesting that these ideals are currently not being followed and in suggesting that in this there is a deep core of systemic racism. The term 'discursive battle' can be used to explain this.

Maly (2014) describes discursive battles as being *"waged over the definition of words, the interpretation of facts, the understanding of the ideology or the general image of the party"*. The BLM movement is waging a discursive battle to let the majority acknowledge that racism is a structual issue in the US and that black people are still being oppressed. Additionally, the movement is waging a battle to show that the state is not protecting the black community and not providing the resources required to improve the lives of black people. The BLM movement is anti-hegemonic in the way that it questions the assumption that black and white people are already equal in the rights they have and in the chances they are offered. Moreover, they also question whether the Civil Rights

Movement has already reached its goal. This sets the Black Lives Matter movement apart from the Civil Rights Movement. The Black Lives Matter movement operates in a different timeframe, where oppression of black people is easier to deny. The reality of a black (former) president seems to counteract the narrative that the Black Lives Matter is pushing, making it harder to put forward the idea that black people are not being treated equally.

Redefining the meaning of certain words is part of waging a discursive battle (Maly, 2014). In line with this, the BLM movement redefines equality: to be equal does not just mean to be equal by law, but to be treated equally by society and to be given the same chances. As Tometi and Lenoir (2015) state: The Black Lives Matter movement is not a Civil Rights movement, but a human rights one. As they state: *"this [the black] struggle is beyond just, "Stop killing us, we deserve to live." We deserve to thrive, and this requires the full acknowledgement of the breadth of our human rights* (Tometi & Lenoir, 2015). The suggestion that the black community is being let down by the government and that a deep-rooted type of racism is still prevalent in contemporary society is inspired by the frameworks set up by the likes of Judith Butler, who suggests that the killings of black people are due to systemic, institutionalized racism in the US (Yancy & Bulter, 2015).

The accusations of systemic racism lead to a counternarrative by opponents of the BLM movement. Opponents of the BLM movement suggest that the inequality that the BLM movement seeks to combat does not exist and they need to "stop complaining". (Peterson, 2015).

[...]

The discursive battle waged by the BLM is not one to get society to acknowledge that black and white should be equal, but rather to get society to acknowledge that black and white are not yet equal. This is one of the important differences between the Civil Rights Movement and the Black Lives Matter movement. Another difference is that the internet has enabled the Black Lives Matter movement to grow quickly and organize itself in a way different from the Civil Rights Movement.

#activism: on Social Movements and New Media Formats

BLM as a (Networked) Social Movement

I discussed what the Black Lives Matter movement is and what it stands for, but have not answered perhaps one of the most interesting questions: how could a movement that started online through the use of a hashtag lead to a nation-wide movement with 30 chapters around the USA? A comparison with the Civil Rights Movement is a useful way to show how social media and the internet enabled the quick mobilization of the BLM network.

The Civil Rights Movement, mentioned earlier in this paper, instantly comes to mind when thinking of social activism by African Americans. This movement was an important for advocate for the equality of black and white people. Often credited as the 'spark' to truly light the fire is the refusal to stand up by Rosa Parks and the following bus boycott throughout Montgomery, led by Martin Luther King in 1955. Similarly, Castells notes that (networked) social movements are *"usually triggered by a spark of indignation either related to a specific event or to peak of disgust with the actions of rulers" (Castells, 2013).* In this way, social movements have not changed much in the digital age: the spark for the BLM movement was a series of black people being killed by the police. What has changed, however, is the speed and efficiency with which a public outcry can morph into a social movement.

Castells (2013) coined the term *'networked social movement'* to describe the new movements that were being enabled by online media. The Black Lives Matter movement certainly agrees with some aspects of the definition of a *networked social movement*. The key of a networked social movement is that it originates online and often has a clear call to action to mobilize indignation (Castells, 2013). In the case of the Black Lives Matter movement, the first call to action was for people to share their stories of discrimination or police violence, further publicizing the hashtag and allowing the movement to grow exponentially. Additionally, the BLM started online and the internet is an important part of the movement. It would be easy to suggest that the BLM movement is a networked social movement and attribute its success to that fact, but the reality is more complicated and the BLM movement differs from Castells's definition of a networked social movement in several ways.

An important aspect of networked social movements is that they are leaderless: they are led by members of the community and are relatively fluid. The BLM movement is not leaderless: founders Alicia Garza, Opal Tometi and Patrice Cullors take on a prominent leadership role in speaking to the media and presenting the 'official' BLM agenda. The BLM movement calls itself a "leaderfull movement", meaning it is led by a collection of local leaders (Black Lives Matter, n.d.). This also points to another way in which the BLM movement is not truly a networked social movement: the movement has a very clear programme, which is presented on the website and consistently communicated by the leaders to the public. This does not agree with Castells' definition of a networked social movement, which suggests that these movements are rarely programmatic. Finally, networked social movements are spontaneous. While the BLM movement started out this way, it has solidified itself as a true organisation that no longer operates purely on spontaneous anger, but rather on a program with clear goals and actions in mind. As the BLM movement itself states: Black Lives Matter is *"Not a moment, but a movement"* (Black Lives Matter, n.d.).

Characterizing the BLM, therefore, can best be accomplished by concluding that the BLM movement is a hybrid between a new social movement and a networked social movement. The characteristics of networked social movements give the BLM movement a strong online presence and a platform for the networked community to interact with one another and to speak out. The characteristics of the more traditional new social movements, such as a clear leadership and program, allow the BLM movement to carry out a strong, singular message and to organize offline actions effectively. It might be that the success of the BLM movement can be found in the balance between a new and a networked social movement.

New Media: Hacking the Hegemony

The features of *networked social movements* that fit the BLM movement certainly aided the BLM movement in growing as fast as it has. An article by Wired, which drew a comparison between the BLM movement and the Civil Rights Movement poignantly illustrates how new media have helped the BLM movement to grow quickly (Stephen, 2016). Stephen (2016) describes the large infrastructure needed to report violence against black people on the streets, during the time of the Civil Rights Movement. Stephen emphasises that it was not the Civil Rights Movement itself that controlled the most important technology and media for their movement: it was the film crews, that were not a part of the movement. They relied on having to use media that were not controlled by those in the movement and therefore, the Civil Rights Movement had to contend with a *Media Hegemony*. New media have turned the tables for social movements like the BLM movement.

New media have enabled social movements to no longer be dependent upon possibly hegemonic mass media, but to express their ideology in their own way, through their own channels. New media, according to Castells (2007), are spaces that are largely beyond the control of governments and therefore allow the flourishing of anti-hegemonic ideas. The hegemonic media monopoly that the Civil Rights Movement had to contend with, is no longer a big issue for the BLM movement. New media, and mainly Twitter, allowed the BLM movement to produce a counter-narrative and become a counterbalance to the hegemonic media and, by extent, hegemonic society. It was new media that allowed thousands of African Americans to share their stories and to show that racism was still a very real problem in the USA. It was new media that was used by BLM supporters to bring to light different instances of police violence against black people. The BLM movement did not need to approach the media to tell the story about discrimination in the USA: they invited black people to share their stories first-hand, on their own platform, allowing the community to write its own story and to shine a light upon issues that had been somewhat left in the dark before.

Furthermore, Twitter, according to Bonilla and Rosa (2015), can be used as a tool for protesting and campaigning in itself. New media and especially Twitter, due to its fast-paced nature, allow the following of events in real-time. Through the hashtag #Ferguson, people could stay up to speed with what was happening in Ferguson and how the community responded to all the events. Livestreams and Tweet-reports enabled what Bonilla and Rosa (2015) call a 'shared temporality'. People tweeting about Ferguson, wherever they were, felt like they were participating in the campaign against police brutaility. The fast-paced access to news, combined with the freedom to contribute to the narrative of a specific issue through hashtags, makes Twitter a particularly suitable platform for campaigns such as the #iftheygunnedmedown campaign. The hashtag #Ferguson, then, was not just people talking about the issue and sharing the news, it was people intentionally making sure the hashtag would be highly visible. It is clear hashtags are often used as a campaigning tool, instead of just as an archiving one.

It is easy to conclude that new media are the holy grail of social movements, and in a way they are. However, there is an important hero for social movements that is often unsung: *Net Neutrality*. This *Net Neutrality* has been a point of discussion for governments for some time and is a crucial part of why new media allow for the growth of social movements. *Net Neutrality* is the idea that the internet should provide equal access to all content, regardless of who produces it or what the ideology behind the content is. It is, in a way, the rule protecting free speech on the internet. This freedom to disseminate any kind of information, be it hegemonic or anti-hegemonic, is important for social movements.

Tufekci (2014) illustrates this by using the Ferguson case as an example to show the importance of *Net Neutrality* for gaining visbility for movements. The hashtag #Ferguson allowed the dissemination of information from a place that would otherwise have been ignored. It drew the attention of the mainstream media to the drama unfolding in Ferguson and allowed the streaming of videos to make this visible. #Ferguson was trending on Twitter, but as Tufekci (2014) notes: it took longer to take off on Facebook. Tufekci suggests that this is due to the algorithmic filtering by Facebook, which makes it a more non-neutral website. Tufekci (2014) suggests that perhaps it was not just the social media, but the *net neutrality* accompanying it, that allowed the Ferguson conversation to grow as it did. It was *Net Neutrality* that was important in allowing the BLM movement to grow, by allowing a financially and socially oppressed group of people to speak out and be visible. With *Net Neutrality* possibly being challenged by the government, one wonders for how long social media will be the free, anti-hegemonic tool that Castells (2007) proposed it to be.

Finally, with the proposed juxtaposition of government, hegemony and mass media against protesters and new media being called into question by president Trump's rejection of the mass media, it will be interesting to see how the shifting relations between the media and hegemony will affect new social movements. With the mass media seemingly increasingly turning against the hegemony, and president Trump utilizing new media to an unprecented amount, the landscape of hegemony and media might see a change again sooner rather than later.

When a #Hashtag Takes to the Streets

Social networks might seem like the dream of any social movement and I just explained how it was indeed these new media networks that allowed the Black Lives Matter movement to exist and grow in the way that it has. It is, however, good to take a critical look at what it means to be a member of an online social movement, and how that translates offline. The term 'slacktivism', coined by

Morozov (2014) describes how 'activists' can take action from their couch by, for instance, sending angry tweets. Morozov calls this kind of activism 'slacktivism': there is no risk involved, no real effort or danger and it ultimately leads to little real action or change. Critics of online activism suggest that this type of ´slacktivism´ erodes the spirit of what it means to be an activist and state that these ´slacktivists´ do not actually promote any change.

While the idea of slacktivism is certainly one to be aware of, the BLM movement seems to not have suffered from it. The BLM movement has been incredibly successful in taking its protests to the street, in mobilizing people. According to Elephrame (2016) there have been over 1600 demonstrations by the Black Lives Matter movement. While some of these protests are made by just one person, many of these are planned centrally, by a chapter of the BLM movement. The BLM movement is successful in mobilizing people, because it doesn't only use social media to allow people to speak out, but also to organize offline protests. This is what Gerbaudo (2012) calls *choreography of assembly*. Gerbaudo (2012) suggests that social media reconstruct how social media are thought of as a tool for collective action, by setting dates and providing instructions for protesters. In this way the social network becomes more grounded in the real world, which enables the movement to 'step out' into the offline world. Gerbaudo (2012) also suggests that social movements online are in fact not leaderless, but are led by so called 'choreographers', who set the scene for people to act in. I previously discussed that the BLM movement is not a leaderless movement, and I suggest that it is because of this that the choreography of the BLM movement could be carried out in a clear and structured manner, allowing for the many big protests that swept the country wave by wave.

The BLM movement has used new media to organize protests. Facebook events is an important tool for the BLM movement. The Facebook page of the BLM movement and its separate chapters show the events and protests, and when and where they will happen. In terms of a choreographed routine: they provide a stage and a time, but the players who will stand on the stage are not predetermined. The BLM movement website is used in much the same way, providing a 'calendar' with events for BLM protesters to attend, if they want to, and the possibility to start their own events as well. It is this planning that allows thousands of people to come together on a regular basis with just one thing in common: they think black lives are important and are willing to participate in events to show it.

It is clear that social media were important in planning the BLM movement protests, but what made people willing to take part in rallies that they knew could have dangerous consequences? I suggest that the reason that so many people were willing to take to the streets for the BLM movement is due to the strong addressivity of the Black Lives Matter movement. Addressivity (Bakhtin, 1984; as quoted by Maly, 2014) means that a message speaks to a certain audience, because of the way the message is formulated or because of the sentiment the message contains. A message tailored to a specific audience will be more addressive and will therefore resonate more with the audience.

The BLM movement is highly addressive to a specific group of people: black people. Research by Charity (2016) shows that most of the people who speak online about the BLM movement are black. This is hardly surprising, but it does illustrate why the movement succeeds at motivating people: because it speaks to people directly. The name of the movement tells black people, who have frequently experienced racism and marginalization, that they matter. It speaks directly to the black community: it is not stating in a vague way that every person should be treated equally, or that racism is bad, or even that it is not real: it's being honest, proud even, in declaring that black people matter. It makes sense that this is a much more personal, mobilizing, address than simply retweeting outrage about an injustice that one is not personally hurt by, to make oneself feel better, which is a type of slacktivism. This time it's personal, and when it's personal people don't slack.

The strong addressivity of the Black Lives Matter movement is amongst the factors that it owes its success to, but it's also what causes it to be highly polarizing. The name of the movement itself seems to somewhat exclude anyone who isn't black in the eye of many opponents, which has caused them to adapt and adopt the Black Lives Matter rallying cry in a very different way. It is the high addressivity of the BLM movement that caused what I term the 'war of hashtags' and the discursive battle of what BLM truly stands for.

The Power of Words: Heroes or Haters?

The BLM movement is involved in a range of discursive battles (Maly, 2014), both online and offline. I already discussed the battle that the BLM movement is waging to show that black people are still being oppressed and are not yet equal. While this is certainly an interesting topic for a discursive analysis, I am focusing on another discursive battle the BLM movement is waging, namely a discursive battle that concerns the very core of the BLM movement. The BLM movement, that characterizes itself as a social justice group, has been termed by opponents as a hate group. The BLM movement is therefore waging a discursive battle over what the BLM movement is at its core.

I discussed before that the high addressivity (Bakhtin, 1984; as quoted in Maly, 2014) of the BLM movement allows it to be highly mobilizing. However, it is also this high amount of addressivity that fuels the counternarrative of the opponents of the movement that the BLM movement is a hate group, only concerned with black people. The slogan "Black Lives Matter" is highly addressive to black people, and therefore it seems to exclude non-black people. This exclusion is even labelled as racism (or 'reverse racism') by some people, such as Perazzo (2016), who compares the movement to the Black Panthers. This, in combination with riots and violence by (supposed) BLM supporters, is being used by BLM opponents to frame the BLM movement as a hate group.

One of these opponents is Spollen (2015), who calls the BLM movement a 'hate group', citing violent Tweets by supporters and accusing BLM supporters of 'laying siege to towns'. Spollen (2015) also describes the effect of a strongly addressive slogan, stating: *"Your life matters. To proclaim that one race's life matters more than another's is inherently racist by definition."* Note that the criticism of the BLM movement does not stem from the idea that black lives do not matter, but from the idea that the BLM movement is problematic as a movement. This narrative is also clear in the text for a petition to classify the BLM movement as a hate group, where it states: *"Black lives matter have endorsed hate and violence against citizens and Police simply because of the color of their skin."* (Hamilton, n.d.). The counternarrative that is created by BLM opponents is one that stresses that the BLM movement only cares about black people and is even anti-white or anti-police. An excerpt from a speech by Milo Yiannopoulos, senior editor for the extreme-right Breitbart news, called the BLM "the last socially acceptable hate group in America." In the speech, totalling a length of 2 hours and 31 minutes, Yiannopoulus discusses that the BLM movement is a hate group and that racism is not a reality anymore.

The BLM movement itself responds to the accusations of them being a hate group by stressing that they do not hate police officers and that, in fact, all lives matter to them. The movement addresses the claim that the BLM movement hates white people in their article '11 major misconceptions about the BLM movement', stating: *"The statement "black lives matter" is not an anti-white proposition. Contained within the statement is an unspoken but implied "too," as in "black lives matter, too," which suggests that the statement is one of inclusion rather than exclusion."* (Black Lives Matter, n.d.). Similarly, the movement states that it does not hate police officers, but seeks to improve the way that police officers interact with the black community. The battle for the identity of BLM has not yet been decided and will doubtlessly continue for some time, with tensions rising during the period leading up to Donald Trump's inauguration as president.

#Alllivesmatter and the War of Hashtags

One of the reasons the Black Lives Matter movement has picked up in the way it has, is undoubtedly its name. The hashtag is short, clear, and strong: it instantly conveys what the movement stands for without needing further explanation. It is hardly a surprise that the format of the hashtag has been adopted by other movements, like #Asianlivesmatter and #Translivesmatter. Where these examples probably come from a place of admiration and willingness to follow in the footsteps of the BLM movement, the BLM movement has requested people not to adapt the hashtag in order to not 'dilute' the conversation, stating: *"Please do not change the conversation by talking about how your life matters, too. It does, but we need less watered down unity and a more active solidarities with us, Black people, unwaveringly, in defense of our humanity"*. (Black Lives Matter, n.d.) The BLM movement suggest that 'plagiarism' of the BLM format can be used to undermine the power that the movement has, which is perhaps exactly why its opponents have chosen to do so in the discursive battle that they are waging.

Two hashtags used by opponents of the BLM movement are '#Alllivesmatter' and '#Bluelivesmatter'. Both hastags were developed in response to the Blacklivesmatter hashtag and have served as a tool in opposing and reframing the BLM message. 'Blue lives Matter' even became a movement itself, advocating the importance of law enforcement and the right for police officers to be protected (Blue Lives Matter, n.d.). The borrowing of the format used by the BLM movement (Xlivesmatter) is a clever trick by the movement to reframe the statements made by the BLM movement. The BLM movement does not state that police lives do not matter, nor do they advocate for violence, as I discussed earlier, but by pitting the term 'Blue lives matter' directly against the BLM movement, the counter-movement suggests that the BLM movement does in fact advocate violence against police officers. The hashtag #Bluelivesmatter is used to change the meaning of the #Blacklivesmatter movement, by suggesting it means '#ONLYblacklivesmatter'. This is in line with the discursive battle that is going on and the counternarrative that the BLM is a hate-group that hates police officers.

The #Alllivesmatter hashtag is similar to the Bluelivesmatter hashtag and is perhaps a stronger opposing hashtag than the bluelivesmatter one. The alllivesmatter hashtag seems to give those who follow it the moral high ground over the BLM supporters. It furthers the narrative that the BLM movement does not care about the lives of those who are not black. The #Alllivesmatter hashtag also furthers the narrative that black people are already equal and that there is no structual racism present in US society. As Butler (2015) puts it: *"If we jump too quickly to the universal formulation, "all lives matter," then we miss the fact that black people have not yet been included in the idea of "all lives."* (Yancy & Bulter, 2015). The 'Alllivesmatter' hashtag, according to BLM supporters, distracts from the message made by the BLM movement and is therefore a strong, yet subtle, weapon in the discursive battle being waged against the BLM movement.

Concluding: Where Do We Go from Here?

The Black Lives Matter movement is a movement in contemporary US society that is as polarizing as it is powerful. In this paper I discussed the history and ideology of the Black Lives Matter movement, as well as why the movement managed to be as successful as it has been and continues to be. I also touched upon the discursive battle that the BLM is waging with its opponents and the war of hashtags being waged on Twitter.

I propose that the BLM movement has combined the features of new social movements and networked social movements with strong addressivity in order to gain visibility and mobility. The BLM movement has shown how the internet can enable public outrage to grow into a structured and powerful social movement. With the political landscape in the US changing dramatically with the presidency of Donald Trump and net neutrality being threatened, the future of the BLM movement is as of yet uncertain. It is difficult to predict where the Black Lives Matter movement will go from here, but one thing is clear: the internet should not be underestimated as a tool for mobilizing outrage, for better or for worse.

References

Black Lives Matter (n.d.) *#SayHerName: A Reflection from Mary Hooks, BLM: Atlanta.*

Black Lives Matter (n.d.) *11 Major Misconceptions About the Black Lives Matter Movement.*

Black Lives Matter. (n.d.). *About the black lives matter movement*

Black Lives Matter (n.d.) *Guiding principles*

Black Lives Matter (n.d.) *Herstory*

Blommaert, J. (2005). *Discourse: A critical introduction.* Cambridge University Press.

Blue Lives Matter (n.d.) *Organisation.*

Bonilla, Y., & Rosa, J. (2015). # Ferguson: Digital protest, hashtag ethnography, and the racial politics of social media in the United States. *American Ethnologist, 42,* 4-17.

Castells, M. (2007). Communication, power and counter-power in the network society. *International journal of communication, 1*(1), 29.

Castells, M. (2013). *Communication power.* OUP Oxford.

Charity, J. (2016). *How #BlackLivesMatter Turned Hashtags Into Action.* Complex UK.

Day, E. (2015). *#BlackLivesMatter: the birth of a new civil rights movement. The Guardian.*

Elephrame. (2016). *Read this list of 1,620 Black Lives Matter protests and other demonstrations.*

Gerbaudo, P. (2012). *Social media and the choreography of assembly: Findings from a comparative research.* Tweets and the Streets.

Hamilton, M. (n.d.). *Colorado Governor: Label Black Lives Matter a Hate Group!*

Lempert, M. and Silverstein, M. (2012). *Creatures of politics.* 1st ed. Bloomington, Ind.: Indiana University Press.

Maly, I. (2014). New media, new resistance and mass media,

Maly, I. (2016). 'Scientific' nationalism. *Nations and Nationalism, 22*(2), 266-286.

Miller, R. W. (2016). *Black Lives Matter: A primer on what it is and what it stands for.* USA TODAY. Last retrieved on 4/12/2016.

Morozov, E. (2011). *The net delusion.* 1st ed. New York: Public Affairs.

Perazzo, J. (2016). *The Profound Racism of 'Black Lives Matter'.* Frontpage Mag.

Peterson, J. (2015). *'White Privilege' Is Not What Is Holding Blacks Back Today.* CNS News.

Spollen, A. C. (2015). *Black Lives Matter Has Morphed Into A Hate Group. It's Time To Treat It As Such.* IJR.

Stephen, B. (2016). *How Black Lives Matter Uses Social Media to Fight the Power.* [online] WIRED. Last retrieved on 4/12/2016

Tometi, O. & Lenoir, G. (2016). *Black Lives Matter Is Not a Civil Rights Movement.* TIME.com

Tufekci, Z. (2014). What Happens to #Ferguson Affects Ferguson: – The Message. Medium.

Yancy, G. & Butler, J. (2017). *What's Wrong With 'All Lives Matter'?.* Opinionator

4

Bernie Sanders's Populism Versus Racial Justice

Dara Lind

Dara Lind is a staff writer for Vox.com, where she covers issues pertaining to immigration and criminal justice. She also worked as a senior policy associate at America's Voice.

This viewpoint describes the tensions between Bernie Sanders's campaign and the movement for racial equality and justice. Critics of Sanders claim he has paid insufficient attention to issues directly affecting the black community such as mass incarceration and police shootings. To Black Lives Matter activists and allies, racial concerns should not be subsumed by economic concerns. The Sanders campaign responded to this pressure by integrating demands into his platform while asserting that they are the natural advocates of racial equality—at least more so than Hillary Clinton or the Republicans. Still, uniting white progressives and left-leaning people of color is a challenge.

O n Saturday, activists affiliated with the Black Lives Matter movement interrupted a Bernie Sanders rally in Seattle to criticize his campaign for paying insufficient attention to issues of criminal justice and race.

Sound familiar? Something similar happened last month at the progressive conference Netroots Nation: Black Lives Matter

"Black Lives Matter vs. Bernie Sanders, Explained," by Dara Lind, Vox Media, Inc., August 11, 2015. Reprinted by permission.

protesters interrupted a town hall meeting with Sanders and fellow Democratic presidential candidate Martin O'Malley.

The activists didn't feel that Sanders—and, just as importantly, his supporters—are keeping racial justice front and center. Sanders has become a progressive hero for his economic populism, but at the beginning of his campaign he talked about racial inequality, if at all, as a symptom of economic inequality.

To Black Lives Matter activists and sympathizers, who've spent the last year or more calling attention to the deaths of young black men and women (many at the hands of police), Sanders's attitude toward race was all too familiar: Generations of white progressives have kept economic issues at the center of progressivism and issues that affect mostly nonwhites at the margins. They've challenged Sanders to make racism and mass incarceration as important to his campaign as Social Security.

Sanders's campaign has clashed with activists over their tactics, but it's been receptive to their demands: Sanders is working to show that he's the candidate of all progressives, not just some of them. Yet many of his supporters are tremendously pissed off at the activists for targeting Sanders, who they see as a natural ally of the movement, rather than going after Hillary Clinton or Republicans.

This is really just the latest mutation of an ongoing conflict. Right now, the two sides are Black Lives Matter activists and Bernie Sanders supporters. But white economic progressives and left-leaning activists of color have been struggling over what it means to be a progressive for decades.

Over the past 20 years, both within the Democratic Party and outside of politics, the vision of progressivism that's attracted the most energy and organizing strength has been a progressivism of identity: recognizing the different ways that various groups are marginalized, and working to reduce those disparities both in policy and in everyday interactions. But many progressives in the Democratic Party are inheritors of a labor-liberal progressive tradition that is primarily worried about economic inequality, and are most excited by economic populists like Sanders and Elizabeth Warren.

Sanders supporters see it as obvious that their candidate's platform would be better for people of color than any other candidate's, and they don't understand what else supporters would want. But for the activists challenging Bernie Sanders and his supporters, it's not enough for progressives or Democrats to call for policies that they think would help people of color—they need to be listening to and incorporating the agendas of people of color themselves.

Bernie Sanders's Economic Populism Is at the Heart of His Appeal

Bernie Sanders has become a surprisingly serious candidate for the Democratic presidential nomination in 2016 by appealing to progressives through economic populism. He's generating tons of excitement; his campaign followed up a 15,000-person rally in Seattle on Saturday with a 28,000-person one in Portland on Sunday.

Sanders was a civil rights activist in the 1960s. But as a politician, he's typically seen racial inequality as a symptom and economic inequality as the disease. The difference between his position and that of other Democratic politicians has become clear over the last year, as politicians and the public have started paying a lot of attention to the deaths of young black men and women at the hands of police or in police custody.

So when Sanders was interviewed by Wolf Blitzer in early May, during the unrest in Baltimore sparked by the death of Freddie Gray in police custody, he emphasized youth unemployment as the "long-run" solution: "In the neighborhood where this gentleman lives [sic], as I understand it, the unemployment rate is over 50 percent, over 50 percent. What we have got to do as a nation is understand that we have got to create millions of jobs, to put people back to work, to make sure that kids are in schools and not in jails."

How Have Black Lives Matter Activists Clashed with Sanders?

In July, Black Lives Matter activists made it clear that they were dissatisfied with Sanders's approach to race during the progressive Netroots Nation conference, when Martin O'Malley and Sanders appeared at a town hall event hosted by immigration activist and journalist Jose Antonio Vargas.

Protesters interrupted O'Malley, took the stage, and gave speeches about the deaths of young black men and women in police custody—ending with a call for both O'Malley and Sanders to present "concrete actions" for racial justice, and to pay tribute by name to women killed by police or who died in custody.

Sanders was defensive and cranky: "I've spent 50 years of my life fighting for civil rights. If you don't want me to be here, that's okay." The protesters were unimpressed. "Your 'progressive' is not enough," Patrisse Cullors, a co-founder of Black Lives Matter and one of the protesters who took the stage, told the press as a message to Sanders and other presidential candidates. "We need more." The next day, at an event in Houston, Sanders mentioned Sandra Bland (who died in police custody in July) and talked at more length about the issue than he had in the past.

At a Defend Social Security rally in Seattle on Saturday, the pattern repeated itself: Activist Marissa Johnson leaped on stage, approached the microphone, and addressed the audience and Sanders alike. After calling for four and a half minutes of silence for the one-year anniversary (which was Sunday) of the killing of Michael Brown in Ferguson, Missouri, she challenged Sanders again on his lack of a concrete policy to address racial violence— contrasting him with O'Malley, who released a relatively detailed criminal justice platform at the beginning of August.

Sanders stood by silently during Johnson's speech. Attendees weren't so quiet: They booed Johnson, and some called for her arrest. Eventually, according to MSNBC, event organizers made the decision to shut down the event, without Sanders getting a chance to deliver most of his speech.

What Do the Protesters Want from Sanders?

This conflict is playing out on two different levels, and the people who are most upset about what happened in Seattle over the weekend, or what happened at Netroots Nation last month, tend to focus on only one of them.

On one level: Activists are targeting Democratic presidential candidates to ensure that their platforms and campaigns incorporate issues of race and criminal justice. When they've targeted candidates, like at Netroots and in Seattle, they've done so to make particular demands for policy platforms. At Netroots, Cullors demanded, "I want to hear concrete actions. I want to hear an action plan." And in Seattle, Johnson reiterated that request: "Bernie, you were confronted at Netroots by black women [...] you have yet to put out a criminal justice reform package like O'Malley did."

Their tactics may be unorthodox, but the dynamic is pretty typical of the relationship between "outsider" activist groups and candidates during primary elections. Activists aren't exactly challenging candidates to earn their votes; they're saying that in the year 2016 it should be a requirement for any Democratic candidate to discuss issues of race and criminal justice, and challenging candidates to meet that minimum.

And on that level, things are going pretty smoothly. Since the confrontation last month at Netroots, Sanders and his campaign have clearly been working hard to meet activists' demands. At a rally in Houston the day after Netroots, Sanders addressed the death of Sandra Bland in police custody. On Sunday night, after the Seattle event, Sanders's campaign released a draft platform for racial justice, which addressed mass incarceration, policing, and voting rights as well as economic issues.

Activists Are Also Targeting Sanders as a Way to Target Sanders Supporters

Bernie Sanders's campaign has, for the most part, been responsive to protesters and critics. Many of Bernie Sanders's supporters— especially on social media—have not. As Roderick Morrow, a podcaster and Twitter personality who started a joke #BernieSoBlack hashtag on Twitter after the Netroots confrontation, explained to me in July:

> [T]here's all these people who, I don't know, they're just sitting around searching his name on Twitter or something, they just come and get in your mentions and start harassing you, they start saying the same things over and over to you[...] it's almost as if they're trying to say, "You shouldn't expect him to continue this" or, "Because he's done stuff in the past, you shouldn't question him now." I thought it was happening to just a few people— apparently it's happening to a lot of us.

Some Sanders supporters attending the Seattle event booed the protesters taking over the stage, and some even called for them to be arrested (which, as Black Lives Matter supporters point out, would be exactly the kind of aggressive policing they're trying to wake supporters up to). And after Seattle, some progressive media outlets are getting frustrated with the continued challenges to Sanders. Gawker's Hamilton Nolan wrote Monday that the activists going after Sanders are "pissing on their best friend."

This is the second level that protesters are attempting to address by disrupting Sanders: to get through to his fans.

Morrow and others see this as a continuation of a longstanding dynamic within the self-identified "progressive movement." White progressives can often ignore issues that disproportionately affect people of color (like mass incarceration), or treat them as secondary to "real" issues like economic inequality. But as progressives, they think of themselves as defenders of people of color and other marginalized groups—so when they're challenged on their anti-racist bona fides by activists of color, they tend to react with disbelief, defensiveness, or outright hostility.

That's exactly how the drama played out in Seattle. When Sanders took the mic, he thanked Seattle for being "one of the most progressive cities in the United States." When protester Marissa Johnson took it, she responded to the crowd's boos by saying, "I was going to tell Bernie how racist this city is, even with all of these progressives, but you've already done that for me."

Identity-Based Progressivism Is Ascendant in American Culture, but Economics Are Still the Heart of Progressive Politics

In some ways, Bernie Sanders is a throwback to an older version of the Democratic Party: one where labor groups were much more powerful within the party than they are today, and identity-based interest groups were much less powerful. The Democratic power structure has embraced diversity as a goal over the last 20 years.

At the same time—especially over the past few years—identity-based progressivism has been ascendant in American *culture*. The Black Lives Matter movement has gotten tremendous amounts of attention over the past year. College campuses are working (with mixed success) to crack down on sexual assault in response to progressive demands. Corporations are showing off their support for same-sex marriage on social media; Caitlyn Jenner's coming out as transgender got her an award from ESPN for courage. And many of these changes are the result of activists targeting corporations, media companies, and other entities in the same way they'd target politicians. (Just think of the campaigns earlier this summer asking companies to cut ties with Donald Trump over his comments about Mexican immigrants.)

But the nexus of these two—progressive politics within the Democratic Party—is something of an exception to these trends. Many progressive voters are deeply worried about economic inequality, and about the domination of both the economy and politics by the superrich. To their minds, this is the existential crisis facing the country. Before the presidential election, the foremost progressive champion in Democratic politics was Massachusetts Sen. Elizabeth Warren, whose entire political career has been built on taking on the financial industry. And Sanders is now generating Warren-like levels of excitement for his outspoken socialism. Remember, the rally he was holding in Seattle—during the weekend that marked the one-year anniversary of the death of Michael Brown in Ferguson—was about defending Social Security. That doesn't mean Sanders or his supporters didn't care about Ferguson, of course, but it is a choice of emphasis.

The Democratic progressives rallying around Warren and Sanders may agree that racial or gender inequality is also a problem, but they may see it (as Sanders long did) as a problem that can best be solved by fixing *economic* inequality. Or they may see them as issues that politicians should address, but not necessarily ones they need to focus on. To nonwhite progressives, especially activists, this makes it feel like "progressivism" is still something for white people.

5

What Is Digital Populism?

Paul Florence and Roderick Jones

Paul Florence is the CEO of Concentric Advisors, the West Coast's preeminent private security, intelligence, and risk consultancy. Former Concentric CEO Roderick Jones is chairman of the board as well as CEO of Rubica, a private network of cybersecurity experts.

The following viewpoint provides an excellent introduction to digital populism and how it functions in an increasingly online world. While populism is not a new set of ideas, rapid new forms of communication and social organizing are transforming how ideas are shared and spread. The Internet has diminished the influence of the so-called elite, such as professional journalists, politicians, and academics. These people used to be seen as experts, but they must now compete for bandwidth with whomever commands the most attention, regardless of merit. While some see this as ideal, other worry it has undermined our institutions as well as our democracy.

A year ago, we warned that in 2016 we would see the "Return of History." It's not only back, but it returned with a vengeance this year, culminating in populist eruptions that are likely to fundamentally alter the international order.

Populism itself isn't new. What is new is the rapid acceleration of communication cycles that facilitated this latest iteration, as populist messages spread swiftly on platforms suited to the digital

"Populism in the Digital Age," by Paul Florence and Roderick Jones, Medium, January 2, 2017. Reprinted by permission.

age. The new political medium is not a thoughtful fireside chat, but a tweet—a direct-to-consumer message that relies on marketing strategies more than policies.

Digital populism also circumvents the elites—journalists, career politicians, and academics. These high priests of Western society have been relegated to voices in the wilderness. While proponents argue that we are witnessing democracy in its purest form, the malleability of our digital platforms actually undermines democratic institutions. In hindsight, we see how easily our national political conversation was exploited by "fake news" and hackers. These platforms are no digital commons of sovereign voices.

In the United States, populism has always been like a geyser; a highly pressurized stream running just below the surface, erupting every 50 years or so. Catalyzed by socioeconomic turmoil, these eruptions reshape the political landscape. Populism has emerged from both the left and the right—in the 1840s, the Know-Nothing party grew in response to the huge wave of Irish and German immigration, which was seen as a threat to both jobs and cultural identity. The next populist geyser came 50 years later, this time from the left, when a coalition of farmers, feeling excluded from the Gilded Age, unified under the People's Party in a backlash against urban elites, big banks, and railroad barons. Sound familiar?

The twentieth century saw smaller, but similar populist cycles, and in the wake of the 2008 financial crisis, we were due for another eruption. During the 2016 campaign, it came from both left and right, as Bernie Sanders and Trump upstaged their more conventional rivals to capture the energy of their respective parties. Trump channeled his version into a winning formula—an anti-immigration, anti-free trade version of populism, updated for the twenty-first century, 140 characters or less.

And this time around, it's not just the United States. Within a span of six months, populist movements have toppled governments in the UK, France, and Italy. With the exception of Angela Merkel in Germany, the moderate internationalists are gone. Instead, we are heading into the uncharted waters of 2017 with new leaders at the helm calling for tighter borders, protectionism, and retrenchment.

The populist formula is well established. The appeal lies with individual charismatic leaders, who, when faced with hard decisions, tell us what we want to hear rather than what we need to hear. They vow to bring our jobs back, keep us safe, and restore our national pride, and promise that we won't have to give up anything in return. Like parents who tell us that we don't need to eat vegetables in order to get dessert. Not surprisingly, the resulting policies are a "sugar high." Immediate gratification, followed by the inevitable crash when populist leaders aren't able to deliver on their lofty promises.

So What Can We Learn from the Events of the Last Year and the Rise of Digital Populism?

First, don't be over-reliant on traditional data and metrics. In this age of ubiquitous data, we often confuse information for answers. During the 2016 election cycle, we saw more polls with increasingly complex algorithms designed to shrink the margin of error. And we have since learned that they were almost all wrong. It turns out that yard signs were better than polls in gauging voter sentiment in battleground states. Not only do we not know what to expect from a Trump presidency, but we were betrayed by the metrics that were supposed to tell us it was coming. Going forward, we need to account for socioeconomic and demographic indicators, from commodities prices to life expectancy, to better understand the true complexity of voters' mindset.

Second, expect uncertainty. Digital populism will increasingly challenge many of the paradigms of the last 75 years. Every major Western leader has preserved the protocols of Bretton Woods, operating within a fairly structured global system of great power norms. We can no longer take it for granted that that stable global structure still matters—yet any deviation from this established path could send shockwaves through the international order. As we enter a new political era, we need to adjust our tolerance for uncertainty.

Third, have a plan. Even for many of the most astute political observers, Trump's victory, Brexit, and the other populist surprises of 2016 came as a shock. But we shouldn't be caught flat-footed again, whether by social unrest, tightened borders or presidential tweet risk. We should make contingency plans for any such scenario, in which we explore all our strategic options. Because the lesson of 2016 is that we should not be surprised by anything, especially in the age of digital populism.

6

Social Media, Chaotic Pluralism, and Populism

Helen Margetts

Political scientist Helen Zerlina Margetts is director of the Oxford Internet Institute and a professor of internet and society at the University of Oxford. She specializes in digital-era governance and politics.

In this viewpoint, Helen Margetts uses the Trump and Brexit phenomena of 2016 as a point of entry into a larger discussion of how social media influences personal beliefs and political action. Here, Margetts outlines some of the concepts in her book Political Turbulence. *Although many see the internet as an "echo chamber," Margetts refutes this idea, claiming instead that social media users consume more, and more varied, news online than elsewhere, such as television. She then introduces the concept of chaotic pluralism to chart the diverse and nonlinear ways social media works and how it might be improved.*

After Brexit and the election of Donald Trump, 2016 will be remembered as the year of cataclysmic democratic events on both sides of the Atlantic. Social media has been implicated in the wave of populism that led to both these developments.

Attention has focused on echo chambers, with many arguing that social media users exist in ideological filter bubbles,

"Political Turbulence, Social Media and the New Populism," by Helen Margetts, Marsh & McLennan Companies, Inc., December 30, 2016. Reprinted by permission.

narrowly focused on their own preferences, prey to fake news and political bots that reinforce polarization and lead voters to turn away from the mainstream. Facebook CEO Mark Zuckerberg responded with the claim that his company (built on $7 billion of advertising revenue) did not influence people's election decisions.

So what role *did* social media play in the political events of 2016? There is no doubt that social media has brought change to politics. From the waves of protest and unrest in response to the 2008 financial crisis to the Arab Spring of 2011, there has been a generalized feeling that political mobilization is on the rise, and that social media had something to do with it.

Our book investigating the relationship between social media and collective action, *Political Turbulence*, focuses on how social media allows new, "tiny acts" of political participation (liking, tweeting, viewing, following, signing petitions and so on), which turn social movement theory around. Rather than identifying with issues, forming collective identity and then acting to support the interests of that identity—or voting for a political party that supports it—in a social media world, people act first and think about it (or identify with others) later, if at all.

These tiny acts of participation can add up to large-scale mobilizations, such as demonstrations, protests or campaigns for policy change, but they almost always don't. The overwhelming majority (99.99 percent) of petitions to the UK or United States governments fail to get the 100,000 signatures required for a parliamentary debate (UK) or an official response (U.S.). The very few that succeed do so very quickly on a massive scale (petitions challenging the Brexit and Trump votes immediately shot above 4 million signatures to become the largest petitions in history), but without the normal organizational or institutional trappings of a social or political movement, such as leaders or political parties, they fizzle out. That's the reason why so many of the Arab Spring revolutions proved disappointing.

The Myth of the Echo Chamber

The mechanism that is most often offered for this state of events is the existence of echo chambers or filter bubbles. The argument goes that first, social media platforms feed people the news that is closest to their own ideological standpoint (estimated from their previous patterns of consumption) and second, that people create their own personalized information environments through their online behavior, selecting friends and news sources that back up their world view.

Once in these ideological bubbles, people are prey to fake news and political bots that further reinforce their views. So, some argue, social media reinforces people's current views and acts as a polarizing force on politics, meaning that "random exposure to content is gone from our diets of news and information."

Really? Is exposure less random than before? Surely the most perfect echo chamber would be the one occupied by someone who only read the Daily Mail in the 1930s, with little possibility of other news, or someone who just watches Fox News? Can our new habitat on social media really be as closed off as these environments when our digital networks are so very much larger and more heterogeneous than anything we've had before?

Research suggests not. A recent large-scale survey of 50,000 news consumers in 26 countries shows how those who do not use social media on average come across news from significantly fewer different online sources than those who do. Social media users, it found, receive an additional boost in the number of news sources they use each week, even if they are not actually trying to consume more news. These findings are reinforced by an analysis of data on Facebook, where 8.8 billion posts, likes and comments were posted throughout the U.S. election.

Recent research published in *Science* shows that algorithms play less of a role in exposure to attitude-challenging content than individuals' own choices, and that "on average more than 20 percent of an individual's Facebook friends who report an ideological affiliation are from the opposing party," meaning that social media exposes individuals to at least some ideologically cross-cutting viewpoints: "24 percent of the hard content shared by liberals' friends is cross-cutting, compared to 35 percent for conservatives." The equivalent figures would be 40 percent and 45 percent if random.

In fact, companies have no incentive to create hermetically sealed (as I have heard one commentator claim) echo chambers. Most of social media content is not about politics (sorry guys), and most of that $7 billion advertising revenue does not come from political organizations. So, any incentives that companies have to create echo chambers—for the purposes of targeted advertising, for example—are most likely to relate to lifestyle choices or entertainment preferences rather than political attitudes.

Where filter bubbles do exist, they are constantly shifting and sliding, easily punctured by a trending cross-issue item. Anybody looking at #Election2016 shortly before polling day would have seen a rich mix of views, while having little doubt about Trump's impending victory.

Even if political echo chambers were as efficient as some seem to think, there is little evidence that this is what actually shapes election results. After all, by definition, echo chambers preach to the converted. It is the undecided people who, for example, the Leave and Trump campaigns needed to reach.

According to research, it looks like they managed to do just that. A barrage of evidence suggests that such advertising was effective in the 2015 UK general election (where the Conservatives spent 10 times as much as Labour on Facebook advertising), in the EU referendum (where the Leave campaign also focused on paid Facebook ads) and in the U.S. presidential election, where Facebook advertising has been credited for Trump's victory while the Clinton campaign focused on TV ads. Of course, advanced advertising techniques might actually focus on those undecided voters from their conversations. This is not the bottom-up political mobilization that fired off support for Podemos or Bernie Sanders; it is massive top-down advertising dollars.

Ironically, these huge top-down political advertising campaigns have some of the same characteristics as the bottom-up movements discussed above, particularly sustainability. Former New York Governor Mario Cuomo's dictum that candidates "campaign in poetry and govern in prose" may need an update. Barack Obama's innovative campaigns of online social networks, micro-donations and matching support were miraculous, but the extent to which he developed digital government or data-driven policymaking in office was disappointing. "Campaign digitally, govern in analogue" might be the new mantra.

Chaotic Pluralism

Politics is a lot messier in the social media era than it used to be, whether something takes off and succeeds in gaining critical mass is far more random than it appears to be from a casual glance, where we see only those that succeed. In *Political Turbulence*, we wanted to identify the model of democracy that best encapsulates politics intertwined with social media. The dynamics we observed seem to be leading us to a model of "chaotic pluralism." This is characterized by diversity and heterogeneity—similar to early pluralist models—but also by non-linearity and high interconnectivity, making liberal democracies far more disorganized, unstable and unpredictable than the architects of pluralist political thought ever envisaged.

Perhaps rather than blaming social media for undermining democracy, we should be thinking about how we can improve the (inevitably major) part that it plays. Within chaotic pluralism, there is an urgent need for redesigning democratic institutions that can accommodate new forms of political engagement and respond to the discontent, inequalities and feelings of exclusion—even anger and alienation—that are at the root of the new populism. We should be using social media to listen to (rather than merely talk at) the expression of these public sentiments, and not just at election time.

Many political institutions are in crisis, precisely because they have become so far removed from the concerns and needs of citizens. Redesign will need to include social media platforms themselves, which have rapidly become established as institutions of democracy and will be at the heart of any democratic revival. As these platforms finally start to admit to being media companies (rather than tech companies), we will need to demand human intervention and transparency over algorithms that determine trending news, fact checking (where Google took the lead), algorithms that detect fake news and possibly even "public interest" bots to counteract the rise of computational propaganda.

Meanwhile, the only thing we can really predict with certainty is that unpredictable things will happen and that social media will be part of our political future. Discussing the echoes of the 1930s in today's politics, the *Wall Street Journal* points out how Franklin Delano Roosevelt managed to steer between the extremes of left and right because he knew that "public sentiments of anger and alienation aren't to be belittled or dismissed, for their causes can be legitimate and their consequences powerful." The path through populism and polarization may involve using the opportunity that social media presents to listen, understand and respond to these sentiments.

7

The Spoiler Candidates

Daniel Bush

Daniel Bush writes about national politics for PBS NewsHour's *website and also appears on the* PBS NewsHour *TV program. He worked as a Capitol Hill reporter for E&E News.*

In the following viewpoint, Daniel Bush discusses the role of third-party candidates in national elections. Currently, third-party candidates must poll at 15 percent to be included in debates but face major financial and structural roadblocks in doing so. In the 2016 race, neither Jill Stein nor Gary Johnson hit this threshold, despite widespread voter dissatisfaction with both major candidates. No third-party candidate has won the presidency. In 1992, Ross Perot failed to win a single electoral vote, despite having been admitted to the debates. Third-party candidates are therefore unpredictable "spoilers." As ideological gaps widen, we can expect alternative political figures to attract more support.

I f given the chance, Gary Johnson and Jill Stein would have used the upcoming debates to remind voters that Donald Trump and Hillary Clinton won't be the only presidential candidates on the ballot come November.

But Johnson, a former governor of New Mexico and the Libertarian Party nominee, and Stein, who is running on the Green

Party ticket, failed to qualify for the presidential debates, which begin next week at Hofstra University on Long Island.

The news, which was announced last week, was not a surprise. Neither third-party candidate came close to meeting the polling threshold of 15 percent to participate in the debates.

Nevertheless, in an election driven by voter frustration with the political establishment, Johnson and Stein could still do reasonably well in November—and potentially play a spoiler role in the final outcome, if the third-party candidates hurt Trump or Clinton in critical swing states. The prospect of a solid showing this year highlights one of the most confounding aspects of American politics: the electorate's inconsistent, back-and-forth appetite for third-party candidates.

When it comes to non-major-party candidates, differences in political talent and experience help explain why some perform better than others.

But in interviews, political scientists, strategists and current and former third-party nominees all agreed that structural factors—such as access to campaign cash and media exposure—determine whether third party candidates break into the national consciousness or not.

"It has less to do with the characteristics of the individual candidate, and more to do with how well things are going in the country," said Robert Shapiro, a political scientist at Columbia University. "What it really comes down to is the level of dissatisfaction with government, and whether there's an open space on the ideological spectrum for a third or fourth-party candidate."

In an interview on Wednesday, Johnson argued that voters this election were seeking alternative options to avoid supporting Clinton and Trump. "In this case you've got the two most polarizing figures of all time and space that are the two major party candidate nominees," Johnson said.

Third-party candidates have been shut out of the presidency since the rise of the two-party system in the mid-1800s. The most successful third-party candidates in the past century have capitalized on political divisions within the two major parties that came about as a result of economic and cultural turmoil in the country.

Consider Theodore Roosevelt. In 1912, four years after his presidency ended, Roosevelt took advantage of a split in the Republican Party to mount an independent run on the Progressive Party ticket. Roosevelt had unusually high name recognition for a third-party candidate, but still only managed to win six states and 88 electoral college votes, finishing a distant second to Woodrow Wilson.

The next serious third-party challenger, George Wallace, built his 1968 presidential campaign around a strategy of appealing to white Southern Democrats who opposed the party's embrace of the Civil Rights movement.

Wallace, a former governor of Alabama who was best known for his support of segregation, won a total of five states and 46 electoral college votes. He is the last third-party candidate to sweep a state's electoral college votes, according to the historian Dan Carter, who has written about Wallace and the rise of modern American conservatism.

But all of Wallace's victories took place in the Deep South, in states that Richard Nixon was likely to win in a two-way contest against Hubert Humphrey, the Democratic nominee.

Wallace seized on the racial prejudice of the era to run the most successful third-party campaign since Roosevelt's, but his divisive approach only took him so far. "His main impact was carrying states that probably would have gone for Nixon," Carter said. "In terms of the final vote, he was a regional candidate."

More than two decades later, Ross Perot turned out to be that rare third-party candidate with true national appeal.

A Texas-born billionaire with no prior political experience, Perot used his wealth to run lengthy, chart-laden campaign ads that raised his standing in the polls in the 1992 presidential election, helping him land a spot in the debates with George H.W. Bush and Bill Clinton.

"He was so weird that he captured the imagination. His tone of voice, his style, we'd never seen anything like it before," said Bill Miller, a veteran lobbyist and political observer in Texas.

Perot was a gifted performer. But he also benefited from events at the time that created a unique opportunity for a plainspoken, outsider candidate to step in and challenge the status quo. In 1992, the economy was mired in a recession; Republicans were upset with President Bush for breaking his campaign promise not to raise taxes; and many voters were eager for a change after 12 years of Republican rule in the White House.

"For a third-party person to be successful, there has to be voter anger, and the candidate has to channel that," Miller said. "And that's not easy. That's why most of them are unsuccessful."

That fall, Perot won 19 percent of the popular vote, the second-highest total for a third-party candidate in modern U.S. history (after Roosevelt, who won 27 percent in 1912). But because Perot's supporters were evenly distributed around the country, he failed to win a single electoral college vote. He fared even worse in his second presidential campaign four years later.

The most famous American third-party presidential candidate, arguably, is Ralph Nader, whom many Democrats still blame for the outcome of the 2000 presidential race.

Running as a Green Party candidate, Nader received 2.7 percent of the popular vote, a fraction of George W. Bush and Al Gore's support. But Nader won about 97,000 votes in Florida, which Bush ultimately carried by just 537 votes after a recount battle that reached the Supreme Court.

Nader's critics have long argued that Gore would have also won the state of New Hampshire, and avoided a recount, if Nader had not been on the ballot and a majority of the state's Green Party supporters had backed the Democratic nominee.

Nader defended his 2000 campaign in an interview on Monday in New York, arguing that the race in Florida was decided by the thousands of Democratic voters who crossed party lines to support Bush.

In reflecting back on that race, and his subsequent, less-controversial White House bids in 2004 and 2008, Nader blamed the two major parties and the media for making it difficult for third-party candidates to compete in presidential elections.

"Here's the interesting thing when you don't get media," said Nader, who sat for an interview in between promotional stops for a new book, "Breaking Through Power." "I was probably known by 80 percent of the people as a consumer advocate. And I think 80 percent of the people didn't even know I was running."

Nader cited a study in a book by the academics Stephen Farnsworth and S. Robert Lichter that found he received just three minutes of speaking time on the evening news shows of the three major broadcast networks between Labor Day and Election Day in 2000. During that same time period, ABC, NBC and CBS broadcast a combined 53 minutes of uninterrupted speech by Gore, and 42 minutes by Bush.

Farnsworth, one of the report's co-authors and a political science professor at the University of Mary Washington, confirmed the statistics in a phone interview.

"What's very clear is that reporters focus on the two major-party candidates. So if you're a third-party candidate and you don't posses the vast personal fortune of a Ross Perot, you're going to be ignored," Farnsworth said. "Presidential candidates who do not have a D or R after their name are finished before they even start."

Terry Holt, a former top Bush campaign adviser, argued that Nader wasn't a factor in the race. "There's always an undercurrent of dissatisfaction with the major party candidates," Holt said. "Al Gore had a weak spot in his base of support that he could never close."

In the interview with PBS NewsHour, Nader, who is 82, focused on the media's role in covering third-party presidential candidates. But he also acknowledged that he could have chosen to run more traditional campaigns that centered on a few signature issues.

"My problem is, I ran on too many issues," he said. "People would say, 'Narrow the issues.' And I would say, 'No, I don't want to. I want to make a declaration.'"

Johnson and Stein have largely followed Nader's make-a-declaration approach in 2016. It may not have gotten them into the debates, but Johnson is averaging around 8 percent in national polls, and Stein is polling around three percent. In one Quinnipiac University survey earlier this month, they polled a combined 17 percent—nearly the total Perot received on Election Day in 1992.

Johnson is drawing support from Democrats and Republicans, though some polls show that a majority of his backers are Republican, a sign that he could hurt Trump more than Clinton. In a recent CBS/NYT poll, for instance, Johnson received 13 percent support from likely voters. Among that group, 8 percent said they leaned Republican, compared to 6 percent who said they leaned Democratic.

With seven weeks left in the race, it's still too early to tell what the third-party effect will be. But if Johnson, who is polling better than Stein, maintains his current level of support, he could change the outcome in some key battleground states.

In Florida, Clinton and Trump were tied at 43.3 percent in a national average of polls taken in the first three weeks of September. Johnson averaged 6 percent, more than enough to sway the race towards one of the major party nominees. Johnson is currently polling at roughly 8 percent in Ohio, another crucial swing state that has tightened in recent weeks.

Johnson claimed that he would finish much higher if he had qualified for the debates. "Ross Perot was polling lower than I am right now when he was allowed into the debates," Johnson said in his interview with PBS NewsHour. "And when he was allowed into the debates at one point he was actually leading in that race."

But experts cautioned that many polls inflate the public's support for third-party candidates.

"In a poll, the voter is offered the candidates' names; this isn't the same thing as what a random voter may know," Micah Sifry, the author of "Spoiling for a Fight: Third-Party Politics in America", wrote in an email.

He added, "while many voters may be unhappy with the choice of Trump or Clinton, not that many are aware of Johnson or Stein, because they have little money or visibility. That's why typically third-party presidential candidates always underperform their polling."

Sifry noted that Perot was the sole exception.

Robert Shapiro, the political scientist at Columbia University, said that future presidential races could feature more third-party candidates if the two major parties continue to grow further apart.

"The one thing that's been happening since the 1970s is increasing polarization and divergence between the parties," he said. "The Republican Party is becoming a consistently conservative party and the Democratic Party is becoming consistently liberal, leaving an opening in the middle."

But Shapiro said that doesn't guarantee the next generation of third-party candidates will be any more successful than the last.

"What makes it imprecise is that you don't know what would happen if [third party candidates] weren't on the ticket. Would people vote for the mainstream candidates or not vote at all?" he said. "There's no science."

8

A History of Third Parties

Freeman Stevenson

Freeman Stevenson served as writer and editor for DeseretNews. com and has also freelanced for outlets like KSL.com and ARANews. com. In 2016, He spent ten months in Syria as part of a Kurdish militia unit fighting ISIS.

In the following viewpoint, Freeman Stevenson looks back over the history of third parties in America. The first third party was the Anti-Masonic Party, which, perhaps due to its limited scope, failed to make a national impact. Other third parties such as the Know-Nothings, North American Party, and regionally split Democrats fared poorly as well. In 1892, the Populist Party united progressives around the country and did slightly better at the polls, as did Theodore Roosevelt in his third-party run. Today, the conservative base that the Tea Party faction represents could split and therefore weaken the Republican Party.

After an open battle between different factions of the GOP during the government shutdown, there is some speculation that the more right-wing tea party will split from the GOP to form its own third party.

Due to the so called "spoiler effect" third parties tend to have on elections in a winner-take-all system—which the U.S. has—it

"Party Politics 101: A Look at Political History of Third Parties in America," by Freeman Stevenson, Deseret News, October 22, 2013. Reprinted by permission.

would not be the first time that a third party made waves in the United States.

Though no third party has ever managed to get a president elected, third parties can have dramatic effects on an election, and indeed the very political foundation of the country. They can cause the major parties to adapt and to change or bring them crashing down around them.

Here's a look at some third parties in the U.S. and the effects they have had.

The First Third Party—the Anti-Masonic Party

Founded in 1828 amidst growing mistrust of Freemasons and their "elitist" control over the mechanics of government, the Anti-Masonic Party is considered the nation's first third party.

Officially the party only had a single platform: dislike of Freemasons. Although its attempts to become a national leading party on this single issue obviously failed, it nevertheless did gain support in the New England area, enough to gain two governors — William A. Palmer of Vermont and Joseph Ritner of Pennsylvania.

Though the party faded and was absorbed into the emerging Whig Party after roughly a decade, the Anti-Masonic Party managed to leave its mark on the election cycle in the United States, being the first party to implement party conventions and party platforms.

William Wirt—the First Prominent Third-Party Presidential Candidate

The Anti-Masonic Party held the nation's first nominating convention in the 1832 presidential election and nominated Attorney General William Wirt as its candidate.

This was slightly ironic as Wirt was himself a former Mason who stated that he had no personal issues with Masons.

Nevertheless, Wirt managed to take Vermont and 7.8 percent of the popular vote in the general election, becoming the first member of an organized third party to win a state in a presidential election.

The 1856 Election

In 1856, the Whig Party, one of the two main parties in the United States for 20 years, collapsed on itself after issues such as slavery, immigration and states' rights proved irreconcilable within the party. Mixed in with the fact that the Democratic Party publicly threw out President Franklin Pierce in the middle of his term, the U.S. had the setting for one of its most interesting races in history.

Parties such as the American "Know-Nothing" Party, Southern Democrats, Republicans and the North American Party all competed on the national stage.

Although at the beginning of the race the Know-Nothing Party was considered the prime opposition to the Democrats, by the time the election was over its candidate, former President Millard Fillmore, only managed to win Maryland and 22 percent of the popular vote. The Republicans under John C. Fremont ended up winning 33 percent of the vote and 11 states, but because of the split, the Democrats under James Buchanan managed to win the presidency with 45 percent of the vote.

The 1860 Election

Things only got worse for the 1860 election, this time with the Democratic Party suffering from hemorrhage between Northern and Southern Democrats, leading to multiple split off Democratic parties.

The Southern Democratic Party split off from the Democratic Party and gave the strongest electoral showing of any third party in U.S. history, gaining 18 percent of the popular vote, 72 electoral votes and 11 Southern states for its candidate, John C. Breckinridge. This left Democratic nominee Stephen A. Douglass with 30 percent of the popular vote but only winning one state and 12 electoral votes.

In fact, not one but two third parties would outperform one of the major parties in this election, with John Bell of the Constitutional Union Party taking roughly 13 percent of the vote but taking three states and 39 electoral votes.

In the end, the Democratic split enabled Republican nominee Abraham Lincoln to win 17 states, 180 electoral votes and 40 percent of the popular vote to win the presidency.

The Populist Party—1892, William Jennings Bryan

As the industrial revolution took hold in America, various pro-labor and agrarian parties sprouted up in the nation. Though these tended to be regional instead of national movements, in 1891 several such parties and groups combined to form the Populist Party.

The party performed well in the 1892 presidential election, managing to obtain 8.5 percent of the vote and 22 electoral votes and four states in the 1892 election under its candidate, James B. Weaver.

The success of the party, and the increasing role grass-roots populism was taking during the turn of the century, led to Republicans and Democrats attempting to woo over the Populist Party.

The Democrats would effectively merge with the Populist Party by the 1896 elections, with William Jennings Bryan being a Populist-endorsed candidate the Democrats agreed to nominate. Jennings would run for president three times in 1896, 1900 and 1908.

Theodore Roosevelt and the Bull Moose Party

After a four-year hiatus from politics, Teddy Roosevelt found himself dissatisfied with the direction of the Republican Party and his successor, President William Howard Taft. So he started his own party, the Progressive Party, nicknamed the Bull Moose Party for its stubbornness.

The Progressive Party failed to launch Roosevelt into a third term in the 1912 presidential election, gaining 27 percent of the vote and 88 electoral seats from six states. However, the 1912 election does represent the best a third party has ever done.

It is also an example of the spoiling effect third-party candidates can have, with the split between Progressives and Republicans allowing Democratic nominee Woodrow Wilson to win with a mere 41 percent of the popular vote.

The Progressive Party was eventually absorbed by the Democratic Party.

Robert M. La Follette Sr., the new Progressive Party and the 1924 Election

In 1924, erstwhile Republican Robert M. La Follette Sr. was fed up by the lack of progressivism in his party and decided to run on the ticket of the Progressive Party. At the same time, many progressive Democrats were dissatisfied with the Democratic Party, leading to a GOP politician being backed by Democratic voters.

Although he only managed to get one state and 13 electoral votes, Follette managed to get 16 percent of the popular vote and for once didn't cause a spoiler effect, as Calvin Coolidge had a commanding lead of 54 percent of the popular vote and the majority of the electoral college.

This was the last time the Progressive Party waged an effective campaign on its own. Since 1924, progressives have tended to stick with the Democratic Party and its platform.

1948 and 1968, the Last Hurrah of the Dixiecrats

In both 1948 and 1968, "Dixiecrats" ran on separate platforms than the Democratic Party and gained a reasonable amount of success from it. Both Strom Thurmond (1948) and George Wallace (1968) ran as segregationist candidates.

In 1948, Thurmond managed to gain 2.5 percent of the vote, and more importantly 39 electoral votes and carry four states.

In 1968, Wallace won 13.5 percent of the popular vote as the last major segregationist candidate, and won 46 electoral votes and five states. The 1968 election marked the last time a third-party candidate won a state.

Ross Perot, the Independent

In 1992, Texas billionaire Ross Perot funded his own campaign for president, running simply as an independent with no official party affiliation.

Over the previous decades, the impact of third-party candidates and parties had lessened, at least in the public eye, with no third-party candidate carrying a state or even breaching the 1 percent threshold on the popular vote. Perot's campaign on a platform of a balanced budget found widespread support from the voting population, and Perot managed to gain 18.9 percent of the vote but failed to win any states or electoral votes.

Overall, it was the best any third-party candidate had done since Teddy Roosevelt in 1912, and though Perot failed to win any states or electoral votes, he did manage to launch discussion on the federal budget into the political limelight.

The Tea Party as the Next Third Party?

With the recent open conflict in Congress between the "established" GOP and the grass-roots tea party movement, many (including those within the tea party) are speculating that it might be time for the more fiscally conservative branch of the GOP to break away from "the moderates" in Congress and form its own party to better represent its ideals.

While history tells us this would be bad for both the GOP and the tea party, with its chance of winning a national election effectively halved, and its overall chance of it happening slim, it is important to look at the effect third parties can have on the major parties in promoting change of ideals and platforms.

9

Sanders, Socialism, and Political Power

Philip Locker

Philip Locker is political director of Seattle's Kshama Sawant's campaign for City Council and a spokesperson for Socialist Alternative, a national organization in political solidarity with Committee for a Workers' International.

In this viewpoint, Philip Locker profiles the campaign of Democratic presidential candidate Bernie Sanders. After Sanders announced his intention to seek the Democratic Party's nomination for president, the former Independent senator from Vermont raised $3 million in four days, stirring up incredible support. Since Sanders's platform challenged the wealthy class that controls the Democratic Party, Locker recommended he run as an Independent and avoid sabotage. Sanders did not, and he lost the nomination. Still, his forceful articulation of leftist policies had broad appeal and interjected a necessary critique into the business as usual politics of the Democratic Party.

Campaign Needs to Build Independent Political Power

Boldly calling for a "political revolution" against the "billionaires and oligarchs" who have hijacked the political system, Bernie Sanders has launched an insurgent campaign for President. The only self-described socialist in Congress, Sanders explained his decision to run to ABC News, saying "We need a political

"Bernie Sanders Calls for Political Revolution Against Billionaires: Campaign Needs to Build Independent Political Power," by Philip Locker, Socialist Alternative, May 9, 2015. https://www.socialistalternative.org/2015/05/09/bernie-sanders-independent-campaign/. Reprinted by permission.

revolution in this country involving millions of people who are prepared to stand up and say 'Enough is enough,' and I want to help lead that effort."

Contradicting the cynics who say Americans are hopelessly apathetic and conservative, his announcement has been met with a tremendous wave of enthusiasm. In the first day of his campaign 100,000 people signed up to get involved on his website and 35,000 people donated $1.5 million, more than any other presidential contender raised in their first day. By the fourth day of his campaign, an incredible 75,000 people had donated $3 million at an average of $43 per donation. Over 99% of contributions to Sanders were for $250 or less.

This campaign can gain a big echo among the millions who are disgusted by corporate politics that are making the rich richer while living standards for the rest of us are increasingly lagging behind. This is why first the Occupy movement and now the Fight for $15 have won such support across the country. It is also why there is increasing openness to the idea of a "third party" and explains how Kshama Sawant won almost 100,000 votes in 2013 when she was elected as a socialist to the Seattle City Council.

Unfortunately, despite Sanders being an independent member of Congress for the past 25 years, he has declared he will be seeking the Democratic Party nomination, a move Socialist Alternative has argued against over the past year.

Sanders is calling for taxing the rich and big business, a trillion-dollar public works program to create 13 million jobs, a $15 minimum wage, single-payer universal healthcare, stopping the Trans-Pacific Partnership (TPP) and other pro-corporate free trade deals, strengthening union rights, and closing the gender pay gap.

His campaign stands in sharp contrast to the waffling and empty rhetoric of Hillary Clinton and other establishment politicians. He was one of the few members of Congress who voted against the Patriot Act in 2001 and calls for dismantling the NSA's domestic spying programs. He stands for bold action to address climate change, demanding a rapid transition away from fossil fuels towards energy efficiency and renewable energy.

Sanders highlights his opposition to corporate power and the 1%, calling for overturning *Citizens United* and saying that his campaign is devoid of billionaires. On the campaign's website, underneath the requisite disclosure phrase "Paid For By Bernie 2016" proudly stands the addition: "Not The Billionaires."

Sanders' Politics

Socialist Alternative welcomes Sanders' decision to run for President to help create, as he says, "an independent voice, fighting for working families" to "bring the fight to the Koch brothers, Wall Street, and corporate America." His campaign will give Hillary Clinton a much-deserved challenge and will widen the spectrum of political discussion, injecting some working-class reality into the increasingly surreal and narrow parameters of official debate.

Given the overwhelming disgust with status-quo politicians and the weakness of independent left-wing forces, Sanders' campaign has the potential to rally millions against the political establishment and their billionaire masters.

In our view, however, Sanders is making a fundamental mistake by running in the Democratic Party primary. Instead, we have argued that he should run as an independent to help build a political alternative to the corporate-owned political parties. There is a glaring contradiction between Sanders' call for a political revolution against the billionaire class and attempting to carry that out within a party controlled by that same billionaire class.

This contradiction will be posed starkly when Sanders loses the Democratic primary. Sanders has said he will endorse the Democratic nominee, which is very likely to be Hilary Clinton or—if Clinton stumbles badly—another safe pro-business Democrat. This will mean that those mobilized by Sanders will be told to support a pro-corporate Democrat, the exact opposite of a "revolution" against the "billionaires and oligarchs." This could result in the demoralization of those mobilized by the idea of fighting corporate power and the loss of a historic opportunity.

Notwithstanding his mistaken decision to join the Democrats, there will be another path open to Sanders when the Democratic machine blocks him. Sanders should continue running in the general election as an independent to provide working people an alternative to Hillary Clinton and the right-wing Republican. Such a step could open up a completely new chapter in U.S. politics, acting as a huge impetus towards the building of a new political force to represent the 99%.

Such a step would go against Sanders' stated intention and his general political approach, but it cannot be excluded. It will be influenced by how events unfold and how much pressure Sanders comes under from his own supporters demanding that he continue running in the general election rather than endorse Clinton.

Sanders' platform points in the right direction, but as socialists we would go further. For example, Sanders calls for breaking up the huge Wall Street banks, a radical reform which we would support. But far better would be to bring the big banks under democratic public ownership.

While Sanders limits himself to a program of reforming capitalism along the lines of Western Europe, we stand for a fundamental socialist transformation of society. While the European workers' movement won huge reforms during the post-war period, capitalism was not overthrown. Under intense pressure, the European capitalist classes made big concessions in order to maintain their social and political power, but since the end of the post-war boom they have carried out an unrelenting neo-liberal offensive to roll back these reforms.

In relation to more immediate political issues, Sanders needs to speak out clearly in support of the Black Lives Matter movement against racist police brutality and mass incarceration. Also, while Bernie honorably opposed both the Patriot Act and the invasion of Iraq, he has, on numerous occasions, voted for military appropriations. Regrettably, he did not oppose the war in Afghanistan and failed to oppose the recent Israeli massacre in Gaza.

Despite these political shortcomings, Bernie's campaign stands out as fundamentally different from those of all the other business-as-usual politicians running for president. To much of the population which has come of age over the past 25 years, he is "still the most radical politician from the Left they have ever seen."

Building Mass Movements Is Key

To achieve the demands Sanders is campaigning on will require building powerful mass movements of working people. To carry out his platform, Sanders' campaign needs to be strategically orientated towards helping to strengthen movements from below.

Bernie made similar points in an interview with *The Nation's* John Nichols when he argued "a campaign has got to be much more than just getting votes and getting elected. It has got to be helping to educate people, organize people. If we can do that, we can change the dynamic of politics for years and years to come. If 80 to 90 percent of the people in this country vote, if they know what the issues are … Washington and Congress will look very, very different from the Congress currently dominated by big money and dealing only with the issues that big money wants them to deal with."

Sanders also pointed out that "We can elect the best person in the world to be president, but that person will get swallowed up unless there is an unprecedented level of activism at the grassroots level."

Therefore, from a socialist standpoint, strengthening the struggles for economic and social justice will be more important than who is elected president in 2016. The key will be to use the 2016 election to help raise the level of organization, confidence, and consciousness of workers and social movements.

The experience of Kshama Sawant's election is an example of what is necessary to build the forces to run the strongest possible campaign and to win its demands. Kshama Sawant and Socialist

Alternative organized a grassroots force that elected the first socialist in 100 years. Once Kshama was elected, the momentum from her victory was used to build 15 Now, a grassroots organization that mobilized hundreds of activists across the city and worked in coalition with labor unions to push through the highest minimum wage in the country at that time.

But experience has shown again and again that the Democratic Party is the graveyard of social movements. In recent times we saw this when the Occupy movement was brutally repressed by police forces under the direction of primarily Democratic mayors with the assistance of an FBI operating under the Obama administration. Even worse was how the Occupy movement was politically demobilized by elements tied to the Democrats with their appeals to support Obama against the Republicans in 2012. In 2004, the anti-war movement was systematically undermined by the rallying behind the pro-war campaign of the Democratic presidential nominee, John Kerry.

The Black Lives Matter movement, the Fight for $15, and Occupy Wall Street have greatly altered the political terrain on the issues of racism and economic inequality. By comparison, much of the left poured tremendous energy and resources into electing Barack Obama and the Democrats only to see them advance the agenda of Wall Street.

Joel Bleifuss, editor of *In These Times*, argues that "a Sanders candidacy offers American progressives the chance to build the infrastructure for future progressive electoral campaigns ... Unlike the 1988 Democratic primary, in which Jesse Jackson carried 11 states only to have his campaign organization disappear into the political ether, a Sanders campaign is set to build a movement with future electoral capacity. Sanders understands that the organization that coalesces behind him must survive the campaign itself and endure."

We agree that this is needed and possible, but Bleifuss's wishes will not be enough to bring it fruition. To avoid Sanders' campaign "disappearing into the political ether" will require that he continues running all the way through the November 2016 election and does not make the mistake, as Jackson did in 1984 and 1988, of endorsing the Democratic nominee once he loses the primaries. This is the clear lesson from Jackson's shipwrecked campaigns, and we must fight to avoid the same mistake being repeated with Sanders' campaign.

Left Primary Challengers and the Democratic Establishment

Activists need to be realistic in recognizing that the Democratic Party establishment opposes Bernie Sanders and will make sure he does not win the Democratic primary. If necessary, they will use all the tools at their disposal, including their access to big money, the mass media, the authority of prominent politicians, and their control over the party structures.

The history of anti-establishment Democratic Party primary challenges underscores this. The Jesse Jackson campaigns of 1984 and 1988 were the strongest left Democratic primary campaigns in recent history. Jackson's radical, populist campaigns garnered huge support—more than it appears likely Bernie will be able to mobilize—and at one stage appeared to be within reach of winning the Democratic primary. Exactly because of this, the Democratic establishment moved decisively to defeat him.

As Ron Jacobs pointed out in *Counterpunch*, "Anti-Palestinian and big business donors and media commentators took a private comment made by Jackson out of context and splashed it across the pages and television screens of America. Racial code words began being heard in relation to Jackson's name. Soon, his chances of winning the Democratic Party nomination were gone. Instead, the party limped out of San Francisco that summer with the Cold War liberal Walter Mondale as its loser candidate [in 1984]."

More recently we saw how key sections of the Democratic Party establishment acted to break the rise of the populist anti-war campaign of Howard Dean in 2004, instead ramming through the pro-war candidate John Kerry to run a failed campaign against George Bush in 2004.

These examples illustrate how the big-business Democrats who control the party are far more determined to defeat anti-corporate insurgents than they are to stop right-wing Republicans.

On the other hand, as long as Bernie does not stand a serious chance of winning the primaries, he will be welcomed and even encouraged. Even Hilary Clinton recognizes that Sanders will bring enthusiasm and attention to the Democratic primaries and provide them with a progressive legitimacy. Clinton calculates that by Sanders shifting the political debate towards the huge concentration of wealth it will also help to undermine the Republicans electorally.

After Sanders is defeated in the primaries, if he goes on to endorse Clinton (or whoever is the establishment pick), the energy behind his campaign will be directed into "safe" channels which represent no threat to Corporate America. In this way, Sanders' campaign would be used as a convenient "left flank" by Clinton to draw in support from union members and activists who are fed up with corporate politics.

It would be tragic if Sanders' campaign ends up playing this role. Unfortunately, he has indicated he will support whoever wins the Democratic primaries. But there is another path available, which Socialist Alternative will be urging Bernie to take and discussing with those supporting his campaign.

We believe Sanders should not limit himself to the narrow framework of the Democratic Party. Rather than endorsing Hillary Clinton he should continue running in the general election when the majority of workers and youth are paying the most attention.

But to even seriously challenge Hillary Clinton in the primaries, Sanders will need to build up an independent base of support. This means building a campaign based on those people not represented by the corporate politicians: organizing people fed up with Congress, building campaign committees rooted in neighborhoods, workplaces, unions, and social movements like Black Lives Matter and the Fight for $15.

Sanders' campaign could play a key role in bringing together these elements into an organized force that can democratically discuss and debate what policies best represent working-class interests and how to advance those struggles. Such a force would be necessary to continue campaigning in the general election and beyond, or else the momentum created by Sanders' campaign will disappear "into the political ether."

In this way, Sanders' campaign could play a critical role in helping to lay the basis for a new political party, a third party, to provide an alternative to the increasingly unpopular Republican and Democratic parties. A broad left-wing or working-class party would be an organization which brings together different struggles and generalizes from them a common set of interests, a political program.

Bernie himself pointed to such an approach when he told John Nichols "there is no question that the Democratic Party in general remains far too dependent on big-money interests, that it is not fighting vigorously for working-class families ... The more radical approach would be to run as an independent, and essentially when you're doing that you're not just running for President of the United States, you're running to build a new political movement in America—which presumably would lead to other candidates running outside of the Democratic Party, essentially starting a third party."

Spoiler?

Some on the left object that such an approach would end up weakening the Democratic candidate and help the Republicans to win the presidency. The fear of another Republican president is real and understandable. Socialist Alternative wholeheartedly agrees that the Republicans need to be opposed and we in no way want to see them elected.

But the danger of an independent left-wing candidate tipping a close election to the Republicans is far outweighed by the more important need for working people to begin to build their own political voice to represent themselves.

Further, the big-business Democratic politicians have proven themselves incapable of defeating the right-wing policies of an increasingly unhinged Republican Party. Let us not forget that despite the "hope" and "change" of Obama's 2008 campaign, once in power Obama's pro-business policies prepared the ground for Republican victories in 2010 and 2012 by demoralizing progressives and allowing the Tea Party to demagogically tap into anger at the Democrats as the party in power.

Sanders pointed this out when he told Nichols: "[M]ost people have given up on the political process … They think there is no particular reason for them to come out and vote … [Hillary Clinton's] centrist politics … That is not the type of policy that we need. And it is certainly not going to be the politics that galvanizes the tens of millions of people today who are thoroughly alienated and disgusted with the status quo.

"One of the things that I find most disturbing … is that the Democrats now lose by a significant number the votes of white working-class people. How can that be? When you have a Republican Party that wants to destroy Social Security, Medicare, Medicaid, etc., etc., why are so many people voting against their own economic interests? It happens because the Democrats have not been strong in making it clear which side they are on, not been strong in taking on Wall Street and corporate America."

We need to break out of the cycle of Democratic disappointment leading to Republican gains, and begin to build a working-class political alternative to the Democrats and Republicans. If not now, when?

Over the next year the main arena for discussion and debate on anti-corporate politics will be within and around Sanders' campaign. All those forces which recognize the vital need for independent left politics need to orient towards the large audience that will likely gather around Bernie.

Sanders' campaign is heading for a political crisis in 2016, when he will need to choose between supporting the Democratic nominee or continue running in the general election. Socialists need to build the strongest possible base among Sanders supporters in preparation for this debate. A strong left current can mobilize Sanders' supporters to demand Bernie continues running, or lead as much of the campaign as possible away from the Democrats if Bernie insists on endorsing Clinton.

Historic Opportunity for Left Politics

The political system in the US is bankrupt. Even pro-capitalist strategists like the editorial boards of the *New York Times*, the *Washington Post*, and *The Economist* agree their political system is dysfunctional. According to Gallup the approval rating for Congress averaged just 15% in 2014, close to an all-time low. Record numbers are registering as independents.

Sanders points out "there is profound disgust among the American people for the conventional political process ... the frustration and disgust with the status quo is much, much higher ... than many 'pundits' understand."

There is a historic opening for independent left-wing politics. One sign of this was in 2013, when Kshama Sawant was elected as a Socialist Alternative candidate with almost 100,000 votes to the Seattle City Council. At the same time, another Socialist Alternative candidate, Ty Moore, came within 229 votes of being elected to the Minneapolis City Council. This opening is shown again with the enthusiastic grassroots support for Sawant's re-election campaign this year (see www.KshamaSawant.org).

In 2014 Howie Hawkins received nearly 5% of the vote for Governor in the highest vote for a left candidate in New York State since 1920. The 2015 Chicago mayoral elections also showed the openness to challenge corporate politics. Tragically Karen Lewis, the president of the Chicago Teachers Union who had filed as a non-partisan candidate, was not able to run due to health problems. She could have defeated "Mayor 1%" Rahm Emanuel.

Nevertheless, a real debate in the Chicago labor movement opened up about what kind of representation workers need. The election showed the potential for labor unions to play a powerful independent role rather than their current position of surrendering to corporate Democrats.

There are millions of people in the U.S. who are ready for a "political revolution" that rolls back the tide against big business. Instead of dividing these forces by channeling some of those who want far-reaching change back into the Democratic Party establishment and thereby alienating another section completely fed up with both corporate political parties, an independent campaign behind an unapologetic working-class fighter could create the kind of unity needed to challenge the capitalist oligarchy that is strangling our society.

Sanders running independently could help to open the floodgates. Our movement is not strong enough to elect an independent candidate like Sanders in 2016, but more importantly an independent Sanders campaign could change U.S. politics forever, laying the basis for a new third party that could give millions a powerful tool to begin organizing against Wall Street.

If you agree, join Kshama Sawant and Socialist Alternative to make sure this historic opportunity is not squandered. We will be campaigning with Sanders supporters against the corporate politicians while politically arguing for Sanders to run all-out through the November 2016 election, as a step toward building an independent political alternative for working people.

10

Contemporary Populism's Unstable Meaning

Charles Postel

Charles Postel is an American historian specializing in politics, reform movements, populism, and the Gilded Age and Progressive Era. He is an associate professor of history at San Francisco State University.

In the following viewpoint, Charles Postel inquires what, if anything, populism means if candidates as dissimilar as Bernie Sanders and Donald Trump are both called populists. According to Postel, some of the blame lies in the media's overuse of this trendy term. On the level of policy, Sanders overlaps with the original populist movement in America. He favors a progressive income tax, better access to quality health care and education for all Americans, and an infrastructure program that would also aid job creation. By contrast, Donald Trump says whatever is needed to be popular, but the embrace of conservatism necessary for him to gain the Republican nomination ensures his policies will not favor working people.

The headlines tell us that the political campaigns of Donald Trump and Bernie Sanders have opened a new chapter of populist politics. A reporter at the *Los Angeles Times* writes on "the populist sentiment fueling both the Bernie Sanders and Donald Trump campaigns." A pundit at the *National Review* asks if Sanders and Trump are "two populist peas in a pod?" and answers in the affirmative. His counterpart at the *New Yorker* analyzes the

"If Trump and Sanders Are Both Populists, What Does Populist Mean?" by Charles Postel, The American Historian, February 2016 pp. 14-17. Reprinted by permission.

Sanders and Trump campaigns under the simple heading "The Populists."[1] These headlines defy ordinary political sense given just how different these two candidates are from each other. Bernie Sanders is one of the longest serving and consistently progressive politicians in the U.S. Congress, and Donald Trump is a reality TV show host and conservative real estate tycoon whose temperamental political compass points towards animosity against immigrants and women. Whether it is policy, style, or temperament, these two candidates make for strange peas in a pod.

Pairing Sanders and Trump indicates just how flexible the term populist has become and poses the question as to whether populist has any useful meaning and if so, what it might be. A good starting point to answer this question would be to trace back to the historical origins of the term. In the early 1890s the People's party—whose members were known by the quirky nickname Populists, or just Pops—represented a powerful movement against corporate power that demanded solutions to the Gilded Age crisis of inequality. By the measure of this historical legacy, Bernie Sanders looks very much like a populist for the "Second Gilded Age," both in his diagnosis of and solutions to society's ills. By the same historical measure, Donald Trump, with his gold-plated jets and mansions, looks very much like the type of plutocrat the Populists held responsible for the injustices and inequities of their time. This suggests that to understand today's headlines about a populist Trump we need a different historical measure and to examine how some contemporary political commentators have separated the term populist from its origins.

Like Sanders, the Populists called for a political revolution—that is, using the electoral process to create a more humane and equitable society. The Populists believed that corporations held undue influence over elections, the halls of government, and the courts. The resulting injustice meant the destruction of the livelihoods of working people and a rendering of society into a nation of "tramps and millionaires." As for solutions, much of the Sanders' campaign webpage reads from the Populist playbook.

The Populists proposed electoral reforms to squeeze corruption out of the system and to make government more transparent. They pushed for a progressive income tax to make the wealthy shoulder more of the tax burden. They demanded public control and regulation of banking, railroads, and other key industries. They advocated for government investment and currency expansion to stimulate the economy, create jobs, build infrastructure, and provide relief to debtors. They wanted more public colleges and universities and to have them better serve the needs of working people. The Populists pushed all these issues onto the political agenda more than a century ago—Sanders currently has them at the center of his campaign. And he has even endorsed a Populist classic: turning post offices into banks to make inexpensive and equitable financial services available to those with too little cash to be considered worthy customers by the commercial banks.[2]

In drawing a parallel between Sanders and the Populists it should be kept in mind that the People's party represented a coalition. Grain and cotton farmers, coal miners, and railroad workers made up its biggest constituencies. The party also attracted a spectrum of middle class activists, from Frances Willard to Clarence Darrow, involved in women's rights, currency and tax reform, and clean government. Some of these activists called themselves "democratic socialists" much in the same way that Bernie Sanders does today. Henry Demarest Lloyd was such an activist and the similarities between Lloyd and Sanders are striking. Born in New York City and educated at Columbia University, Lloyd became a journalist dedicated to the ethics of social justice. In 1894, the same year he ran as a Populist candidate for Congress, Lloyd published *Wealth against Commonwealth,* a deeply researched study of how the wealth of Standard Oil and other giant corporations undermined democratic government. Lloyd's book inspired a generation of "trust busting" reformers who believed that the very size of the corporate giants constituted a threat to the common good.[3] With his refrain about banks being "too big to exist," Sanders echoes the ethical arguments of *Wealth against Commonwealth.* But here it should be noted that farm and labor Populists did not fully share Lloyd's concerns about corporate size. Instead, they often accepted the principle of the economy of scale and focused on building up big institutions—cooperatives, unions, governmental agencies—capable of matching or surpassing the size and power of corporations.

Not everything about the Sanders campaign is a Populist echo. Sanders discusses saving American jobs in ways that suggest a type of protectionism that most Populists viewed as a corporate handout paid for by farmers and consumers. Or consider civil rights. Sanders speaks forcefully about overcoming the country's history of racial oppression. By contrast, the Populists were silent about this history and complicit in the oppression. At the same time, the People's party did not rely on white supremacist fervor in the way the Democratic party did in the days of Jim Crow, nor did it traffic in the xenophobic passions that were alive in the Republican party. Much as Sanders has done in his political career, the Populists argued that economic reform was the way to solve racial, ethnic, and sectional friction.

If the Populists of the 1890s shed historical light on the democratic socialism of Bernie Sanders, how do we make sense of the claim that Donald Trump is the other populist in the campaign? Here we need to look at the history of a journalistic practice. In recent years, pundits have promiscuously applied the populist tag to political phenomena that escape easy labels and used populist to describe political appeals that are simply popular. In this regard, Trump can be hard to pin down. His policy positions focus on tax cuts favoring the wealthy and draconic measures against undocumented immigrants and Muslims. Beyond that, he seems to ad lib whatever might prove popular and drive up his poll numbers among Republican primary voters. He trades in racial and ethnic stereotypes, insults against women and the disabled, and opportunistic sniping at various elites among TV personalities, hedge fund managers, and politicians. His targets can seem arbitrary and random. From a historical perspective, however, Trump is continuing a long tradition in American politics—a tradition of appealing for the votes of the "common man" by combining tough talk against malevolent elites with ugly scapegoating of marginalized groups. Andrew Jackson rose to political heights as the slayer of both the "monster bank" and "savage Indians." Ronald Reagan demonized both "Hollywood liberals" and "welfare queens." Trump employs the same political arts to gain popularity and he does so in the scattershot style of the reality TV show host that he is.

Trump's campaign has drawn comparisons with anti-immigrant and nationalist parties in Europe. Much like Marine Le Pen's French National Front and Nigel Farage's U.K. Independence Party, Trump gives voice to xenophobia, anti-Muslim prejudice, and aggrieved nationalism. Such politicians carry the moniker of "right-wing populists" in the European media. Le Pen and Farage are called right-wing because they claim the conservative heritage of the ideological and political right as it has been understood since the days of the French Revolution. And the European media uses the term populist to describe, among other features, how such politicians appeal to the "people" in the face of perceived threats to the nation. By comparison, Trump usually does not speak in the name of the "people" in the same way. He flaunts his billions, sneers at the people who are "losers" and whose wages are "too high," and promises to make the country "great again" by the sheer power of his wealth and business acumen. Moreover, somewhat ironically, unlike Le Pen and Farage, Trump does not have deep roots in right-wing or conservative politics. But that is changing. [4]

In the course of his campaign, Trump has been steadily moving towards the conservative orthodoxy demanded by many of today's Republicans. By seeking the Republican nomination, he has had to adhere to most of the conservative principles with which most voters in Republican primaries align. This points to another journalistic practice. In recent years, even when politicians declare themselves conservatives and that easy label fits best, commentators often prefer to use the adjective populist instead. They may do this because the current ambiguity of the term provides a bit of protection from charges of ideological bias. Or the term may have cachet that attracts clicks and sells papers. Whatever the rationale, the pundits who insist that today's self-described conservatives are really populists are reprising an argument that the historian Richard Hofstadter made sixty years ago. Their likely point of reference is Hofstadter's *The Age of Reform* (1955), in which he speculated that the conservative paranoia and witch-hunts of Joseph McCarthy had their roots in the Populist movement of the 1890s. According to Hofstadter, the Populists embraced irrational myths of the past and unreasoned grievances about the present. As a result, he explained, the Populist tradition was unstable, easily shifting from left to right, and thereby "soured" into the intolerance and "cranky pseudo-conservatism" of the 1950s.[5]

In the American context, Hofstadter's thesis of an unstable Populism of the 1890s going "sour" continues to inform journalistic practice. In a 2015 issue of the *New Yorker,* George Packer writes that Sanders and Trump fit the pattern of "the volatile nature of populism" that "can ignite reform or reaction, idealism or scapegoating." He cites as evidence that the Populist Tom Watson of Georgia ended his political career as a racial demagogue. But what if Watson was more of the exception than the rule?[6] What if—as more than half a century of historical scholarship has confirmed and reconfirmed—the great majority of former Populist leaders, activists, and supporters went to their graves committed to their ideals of social justice? Clarence Darrow, like many former Populists, found a political home in the farmer-labor wing of the Democratic party. Others, like Mary Elizabeth Lease, the "Queen of Kansas Populism," did the same in the progressive wing of the Republican party. Still others took the path of Henry Demarest Lloyd and joined the Socialist movement led by the former labor Populist Eugene V. Debs, the same Debs whose picture hangs on the wall of Bernie Sanders's Washington office.

As the decades roll along, the journalistic claims about populist volatility and shape-shifting sound increasingly strange. The political thought that motivated the original Populists has proven to be at least as constant as any other school of political ideas. In its proposals for making a more just and equitable society and under a variety of names—antimonopolist, farmer-labor, populist, democratic socialist, nonpartisan, progressive—populism has remained a steady, deep, and broad stream in American political thought. As of this writing, this stream shows no sign of jumping its banks and turning to the far right, any more than Bernie Sanders is about to sport an orange comb-over and campaign for a new round of tax cuts for the "winners" and billionaires.

Notes

1. Kathleen Hennessey, "The Populist Sentiment Fueling Both the Bernie Sanders and Donald Trump Campaigns," *Los Angeles Times,* August 14, 2015; Johan Goldberg, "Sanders and Trump: Two Populist Peas in a Pod?" *National Review,* August 19, 2015; George Packer, "The Populists," *New Yorker,* September 7, 2015.

2. Joe Pinsker, "Bernie Sanders's Highly Sensible Plan to Turn Post Offices into Banks," *The Atlantic,* October 20, 2015.

3. Chester McArthur Destler, "Wealth against Commonwealth, 1894 and 1944," *American Historical Review,* 50 (October 1944), 49–72.

4. Cas Mudde, "The Trump Phenomenon and the European Populist Radical Right," *The Washington Post,* August 26, 2015.

5. Richard Hofstadter, *The Age of Reform* (1955), 20.

6. Walter T. K. Nugent, *The Tolerant Populists: Kansas Populism and Nativism* (1963); Michael P. Rogin, *The Intellectuals and McCarthy: The Radical Specter* (1967); James R. Green, *Grass-Roots Socialism: Radical Movements in the Southwest, 1895–1943* (1978).

11

The Democratic Party's Empty Populism

Socialist Worker

The Socialist Worker is the International Socialist Organization's daily news and opinion site, based in the United States, with reports from struggles around the world and ongoing analysis of political events.

In this viewpoint, the Social Worker lambasts Obama's hollow populism as mere election year rhetoric. In his 2012 State of the Union speech, Obama acknowledged the widening gap between the wealthiest Americans and the rest of the nation. Although he paid lip service to the Occupy movement and other forces on the left, his record tells an altogether different story. After the financial crisis of 2007, Obama responded with a bailout package that committed trillions to saving the perpetrators of the crisis. His job creation program was abandoned in favor of corporate tax cuts. Like his Democratic predecessor Bill Clinton, Obama proposed, but did not enact, policies that would benefit the lower and middle classes.

Republicans, Democrats, the media—they all agree: In his State of the Union speech Tuesday night, Barack Obama presented a populist economic program that would use the powers of the federal government to take on Wall Street and Corporate America.

That assessment is no surprise from Republicans. They've been raving about Obama's supposed "class warfare" tendencies from the moment he stepped into the Oval Office.

"Obama the Populist?" SocialistWorker.org, January 25, 2012. Reprinted by permission.

But the Democrats are actually singing a different tune. In contrast to other points during his first three years in office, Obama and his party are encouraging the idea that his presidency is crusading against corporate and financial power on behalf of ordinary people.

What's changed? Simple: It's an election year. As his advisers freely admitted to media commentators, Obama's speech was delivered with Election 2012 in mind—to draw a contrast with the multimillionaires and bigots (and multimillionaire bigots) battling over the Republican presidential nomination.

To some extent, the sharper edge in Obama's speech is another result of the rise of the Occupy movement and its impact on U.S. politics. Even mainstream Washington politicians have had to acknowledge the increasingly vocal discontent about a society divided between the super-rich 1 percent at the top and the rest of us.

This shift has been a breath of fresh air, especially considering what was dominating Washington politics before—obsessions about the deficit and the need to cut, cut and cut some more. When mainstream political leaders talk about increasing taxes on the rich and curbing Wall Street greed, even if they don't mean it, this can give ordinary people greater confidence to fight for an alternative to the status quo of austerity.

But there's another fact of history that bears on Obama's speech and can't be forgotten: Democrats always talk more left—at least in relation to the Republicans—when an election is looming.

It's a basic fact of the U.S. political system: The Democrats will say one thing to win votes and do another once in office. And if campaign promises aren't enough, there's always scare tactics—threatening supporters with the consequences of the Republicans in power to get their vote.

Those who care about winning the kind of policies and programs Democrats talk about around election time have to separate the rhetoric from the reality. And when you look at the fine print of the State of the Union, there's less to Obama's "left turn" than meets the eye.

Obama was explicit about growing inequality in U.S. society: "We can either settle for a country where a shrinking number of people do really well, while a growing number of Americans barely get by. Or we can restore an economy where everyone gets a fair shot, everyone does their fair share and everyone plays by the same set of rules.

The first thing to say, of course, is that the U.S. has been "a country where a shrinking number of people do really well, while a growing number of Americans barely get by" throughout Obama's first three years in office—and he bears plenty of the responsibility for that.

When he took office, Obama's Treasury Department adopted nearly wholesale the Bush administration's Wall Street bailout. Literally trillions of dollars were committed to saving the biggest banks and financial firms—with few if any conditions imposed, much less talk about nationalization, which would have been an easy sell to the vast majority of people following the 2008 financial meltdown.

Meanwhile, the administration's help for homeowners suffering the effects of the mortgage crisis has been paltry.

According to a Treasury Department report on the Home Affordable Modification Program (HAMP), as of early January, just over 900,000 borrowers threatened with foreclosure have had their mortgage loans permanently modified under the program. That's a far cry from the administration's target, when HAMP was introduced three years ago, of helping 3 to 4 million households—and even further from the 8 million homeowners who have faced the threat of foreclosure since the crisis began.

Beyond the financial sector, too, Corporate America is enjoying record profits—nearly $2 trillion in the third quarter of last year alone, a new record. The Great Recession is becoming a dim memory in corporate boardrooms.

But not for U.S. workers. The most obvious symbol of continuing tough times is the stubborn hold of long-term unemployment.

The federal government's employment reports did show increases through the end of 2011, including a jump of 200,000 net new jobs in December. But the gap between this and what's needed to reach pre-recession employment levels is enormous. According to economist Heidi Shierholz of the Economic Policy Institute, the U.S. economy needs to add *10 million* jobs—to make up for 6.1 million lost during the recession and 4 million needed to keep up with population growth over the period.

Obama and his advisers recognize that claims about the economy "turning a corner" aren't going to be convincing to lots of people still suffering the impact of the crisis. That's why his State of the Union speech stressed the need for government action to spur job creation.

Of course, the Obama administration knows full well that the president's State of the Union initiatives aren't likely to get through the GOP-controlled House with an election coming up—witness the fate of Obama's proposed "American Jobs Act," which was blocked nearly in its entirety by the Republican-controlled House last fall.

But even if Obama's job creation proposals stood a chance of being enacted, they mainly come in a form that would blunt their impact: tax breaks.

Instead of direct spending on government programs that would lead to more hiring, in both the public and private sector, Obama and his team have focused on tax breaks for corporations, as inducements to hire workers and keep jobs in the U.S.

But U.S. corporations have already returned to pre-recession levels of profitability without new hiring—by squeezing more work out of fewer employees. According to the latest estimate, U.S. corporations have more than $2 trillion in cash and other liquid assets on their books, and they're still not making investments that create jobs in large numbers. The prospect of more tax breaks—at a time when corporate tax revenues have fallen to historic lows—isn't going to be the decisive factor in companies investing again.

By comparison, programs that would be far more effective in getting jobs for the unemployed—like projects to rebuild infrastructure—got short-changed again by the administration.

So even when you take Obama's proposals at face value, they fall short of anything that would deserve to be called "populist," much less "radical."

Keep that in mind when you hear Obama talk about coming down hard on Wall Street fraudsters. In the State of the Union, Obama promised "to create a special unit of federal prosecutors and leading state attorneys general to expand our investigations into the abusive lending and packaging of risky mortgages that led to the housing crisis. This new unit will hold accountable those who broke the law, speed assistance to homeowners, and help turn the page on an era of recklessness that hurt so many Americans."

Sounds good, right? Only the administration reportedly just reached a draft settlement with major banks over their corrupt and illegal practices that plunged at least 1 million people into foreclosure—and the deal is, bluntly, a sellout.

Five of the biggest U.S. banks are involved—Bank of America, JPMorgan Chase, Wells Fargo, Citibank and Ally Financial. Investigators from the Department of Housing and Urban Development and other agencies uncovered evidence of wrongdoing on a huge scale, from the use of fraudulent or faulty documentation during foreclosure processing to bilking the federal government out of billions in inflated reimbursements.

But the banksters have been pressing hard to limit any financial penalties or requirements that they help the homeowners they swindled—and according to media reports, they got their way. The settlement reportedly applies to only a minority of homeowners in trouble on their mortgages—and it would shield the banks from future efforts to make them pay.

The $25 billion total price tag on the settlement may have awed the press, but it's laughably low, say housing advocates. According to social justice advocates Van Jones and George Goehl, the banks should have to pay a minimum of $300 billion to reduce loan amounts for homeowners in trouble or compensate families who were foreclosed on illegally.

If Obama really wanted to confront the ongoing foreclosure crisis, he could push for the banks to be forced to write down the value of every "underwater" mortgage where owners owe more than their homes are worth. According to one report sponsored by a coalition of liberal advocacy groups, this would "pump $71 billion per year into the economy, create more than 1 million jobs annually and save families $6,500 per year on mortgage payments."

Wall Street could easily afford such a measure—U.S. banks are sitting on a cash hoard of $1.64 trillion, and bonuses and compensation are back to pre-recession levels and higher at the biggest financial firms.

But the Obama White House isn't really interested in making the banks pay for the disaster they caused—and so we get another administration initiative touted as a dramatic effort to help working people, which turns out to be nothing of the sort.

The gap between rhetoric and reality isn't unique to Obama. Conservative journalist and political operative David Frum rightly identified the same dynamic the last time a Democrat occupied the White House:

> Since 1994, [Bill] Clinton has offered the Democratic Party a devilish bargain: Accept and defend policies you hate (welfare reform, the Defense of Marriage Act), condone and excuse crimes (perjury, campaign finance abuses), and I'll deliver you the executive branch of government...
>
> He has assuaged the left by continually proposing bold new programs—the expansion of Medicare to 55 year olds, a national day-care program, the reversal of welfare reform, the hooking up of the Internet to every classroom...And he has placated the right by dropping every one of these programs as soon as he proposed it. Clinton makes speeches, [Treasury Secretary Robert] Rubin and [Federal Reserve Chair Alan] Greenspan make policy, the left gets words, the right gets deeds.

The Democrats' say-one-thing-and-do-another deception is inevitable in a party whose popular support depends on claiming to stand up for working people, but whose role in the American two-party system is to defend the interests of Corporate America and the ruling elite.

Any lingering doubts about that role can be dispelled with a look at who's giving Obama money to run for president again.

In 2008, Obama won the corporate money race against Republican John McCain, particularly when it came to contributions from Wall Street banks and financial firms. Once the GOP nomination is decided this year, Wall Street might shift behind the Republicans. But in the early stages of the campaign, Obama had raised twice as much from the finance industry as any Republican, despite all the wild rhetoric about his "class war" against the bankers.

Obama is the leader of one of the two mainstream parties that make up a bipartisan political establishment. That establishment has a left and a right wing, and so Obama's positions and policies at any point will likely be to the left of the Republicans. But people who only look at that difference miss the forest for the trees—they ignore the much greater areas of agreement between the two parties, whether about the necessity of austerity policies or the defense of U.S. imperial interests or the need for repressive laws to limit dissent.

Our movements can't place any hopes in the Democrats, whether they are promising half steps forward—or taking half or whole steps backward. We should fight for what we believe in—and to do that, we need to remain independent of both capitalist parties in the U.S. political system.

12

The Threat of a Networked Public Sphere

Vyacheslav Polonski

Vyacheslav Polonski is a network scientist at the Oxford Internet Institute, specializing in the sociology of the Internet. As the founder of Avantgarde Analytics, he advises senior political leaders on algorithmic election campaigns and AI-powered governance.

In this final viewpoint, Vyacheslav Polonski offers his take on how the Internet has changed the ways in which citizens interact. The speed and anonymity of online communication has transformed the traditional public sphere into a networked one. The free flow of information this network enables is a boon to authoritarian societies where information is tightly controlled, but is it beneficial to a political process for which informed opinions and civilized discourse are required for good outcomes? Online, people curate their feeds and generally only interact with likeminded people. This can amplify and distort views and embolden those expressing hateful and repellent views.

Over the past two decades, the internet has rewired civil society in unprecedented ways, propelling collective action to a radically new level of citizen autonomy.

Democracy is now not only infrequently exercised at the ballot box, but is lived and experienced online on a day-to-day basis.

"The Biggest Threat to Democracy? Your Social Media Feed," by Vyacheslav Polonski, World Economic Forum, August 4, 2016. Reprinted by permission.

Much has been made of the democratizing effect of the internet, and its emancipatory impact on under-represented and marginalized groups living under authoritarian regimes, where it nurtures a networked public sphere that constitutes an independent alternative to tightly controlled media environments.

According to Harvard's Yochai Benkler, this networked public sphere allows for bottom-up agenda-setting, universal access to information, and freedom from governmental interference. Benkler explains: "The various formats of the networked public sphere provide anyone with an outlet to speak, to inquire, to investigate, without need to access the resources of a major media organization."

Since more members of society are now encouraged to participate in public discourse and speak up about matters they deem to be of public concern, the internet has rendered the diversity of citizens' views more salient. This is particularly visible when there is conflict and disagreement between different political or civic interest groups. Whenever there is a controversial policy announcement, there will always be a highly motivated group of people who use the internet to apply enormous pressure on politicians in these moments by voicing their discontent.

Democratic bodies are typically elected in periods of three to five years, yet citizen opinions seem to fluctuate daily and sometimes these mood swings grow to enormous proportions. When thousands of people all start tweeting about the same subject on the same day, you know that something is up. With so much dynamic and salient political diversity in the electorate, how can policy-makers ever reach a consensus that could satisfy everyone? If our representatives are unable to keep up with digital expressions of citizen sentiment, does that mean that we have become ungovernable by the institutions that exist today?

At the same time, it would be a grave mistake to discount the voices of the internet as something that has no connection to real political situations. Last month, British politicians and activists campaigning for Britain to remain in the EU in the recent referendum had to learn this lesson the hard way.

What happened in the UK was not only a political disaster, but also a vivid example of what happens when you combine the uncontrollable power of the internet with a lingering visceral feeling that ordinary people have lost control of the politics that shape their lives. When people feel their democratic representatives do not serve them anymore, they turn to the internet. They look for others who feel the same and moans turn into movements.

In this regard, the Leave campaign's main social media messages appealed to the agency of ordinary voters to reject the rule of the bureaucracy and "take control" of their own country. Using very simple language, largely consisting of only a few syllables, these messages spread very fast across the internet and were often reinforced with amusing memes, instead of rigorous expert opinions or statistics.

Polarization as a Driver of Populism

In light of these recent developments, right-wing populist sentiments have been growing in strength and popularity across both Europe and the US. These movements are fuelled by populist anger, resurgent nationalism, and a deep-rooted hostility towards immigrants.

People who have long entertained right-wing populist ideas, but were never confident enough to voice them openly, are now in a position to connect to like-minded others online and use the internet as a megaphone for their opinions. They become more confident and vigorous, because they see that others share their beliefs. This is concerning, because we know from previous research that increased contact with people who share our views makes our previously held beliefs more extreme. It grants us new group identities that permit us to do things we deemed inconceivable before. In this way, one could argue that the Brexit vote was as much a vote to reclaim one's political independence as it was a vote to reclaim one's lost national identity.

The greater diversity and availability of digital content implies that people may choose to only consume content that matches their own worldviews. We choose who to follow and who to befriend.

The resulting echo chambers tend to amplify and reinforce our existing opinions, which is dysfunctional for a healthy democratic discourse. And while social media platforms like Facebook and Twitter generally have the power to expose us to politically diverse opinions, research suggests that the filter bubbles they sometimes create are, in fact, exacerbated by the platforms' personalization algorithms, which are based on our social networks and our previously expressed ideas.

This means that instead of creating an ideal type of a digitally mediated "public agora", which would allow citizens to voice their concerns and share their hopes, the internet has actually increased conflict and ideological segregation between opposing views, granting a disproportionate amount of clout to the most extreme opinions.

The Disintegration of the General Will

In political philosophy, the very idea of democracy is based on the principal of the general will, which was proposed by Jean-Jacques Rousseau in the 18th century. Rousseau envisioned that a society needs to be governed by a democratic body that acts according to the imperative will of the people as a whole.

However, Rousseau foresaw in Book IV of the Social Contract that "when particular interests begin to make themselves felt [...], the common interest changes and finds opponents: opinion is no longer unanimous; the general will ceases to be the will of all; contradictory views and debates arise; and the best advice is not taken without question."

The internet, in particular, intensifies the fragmentation of opinions, allowing people who are most passionate, motivated and outspoken to find likeminded others and make themselves heard—as we have seen on social media in the EU referendum.

In a similar vein, sudden attention-grabbing focusing events, such as natural disasters, terrorist attacks or external shocks to the environment, could also sway public opinion and trigger hasty political decisions with potentially unsustainable repercussions.

Politicians run the risk of making important policy-decisions based on current emotional bursts in the population or momentary popular opinions, rather than what is best for the country. For instance, important and far-reaching decisions, such as leaving the EU, would need to be approved by qualified two-thirds majorities in multiple plebiscites over several years.

The critical challenge for policy-makers is, therefore, to learn to distinguish when a seemingly popular movement does actually represent the emerging general will of the majority and when it is merely the echo of a loud, but insignificant minority.

Prospects for a Future-proof Democracy

There can be no doubt that a new form of digitally mediated politics is a crucial component of the Fourth Industrial Revolution: the internet is already used for bottom-up agenda-setting, empowering citizens to speak up in a networked public sphere, and pushing the boundaries of the size, sophistication and scope of collective action. In particular, social media has changed the nature of political campaigning and will continue to play an important role in future elections and political campaigns around the world.

However, this technology can also be a platform for conflict and malicious agitation by right-wing populists that are dysfunctional for a healthy democratic discourse, while our current governance systems are susceptible to emotional bursts and populist movements that unfold on the internet. What the EU referendum has taught us is that this accelerating technology is open to all and can be used to influence the public agenda in many different ways. Intimated by the power of internet users, our current governance institutions are, however, incapable of handling the dynamism and diversity of digitally-mediated citizen opinions.

We are thus not ungovernable in the long term, but need to govern ourselves in radically new ways. The only way to accomplish that is by re-imagining the institutions that would allow citizens to engage in enlightened debate in an active and inclusive public sphere.

Organizations to Contact

The editors have compiled the following list of organizations concerned with the issues debated in this book. The descriptions are derived from materials provided by the organizations. All have publications or information available for interested readers. The list was compiled on the date of publication of the present volume; the information provided here may change. Be aware that many organizations take several weeks or longer to respond to inquiries, so allow as much time as possible.

Black Lives Matter
website: blacklivesmatter.com

Founded by Patrisse Cullors, Opal Tometi, and Alicia Garza #BlackLivesMatter is an online forum and chapter-based organization intended to build connections between black people and their allies to fight anti-black racism, to spark dialogue among black people, and to facilitate the types of connections necessary to encourage social action and engagement.

Center for Communication and Civic Engagement
Department of Communication, Room 125
Box 353740
University of Washington
Seattle, WA 98195
phone: (206) 685-1504
email: ccce@u.washington.edu
website: ccce.com.washington.edu/projects/digitalMedia.html

The ways people communicate, to whom, and with what effects are crucial elements of vibrant public life. The Center for Communication and Civic Engagement is dedicated to understanding these dynamic media systems in order to promote citizen engagement and effective participation in local, national, and global affairs.

Democratic Party
430 South Capitol Street SE
Washington, DC 20003
phone: (202) 863-8000
website: www.democrats.org

There are several core beliefs that tie the Democratic Party together: That Democrats are greater together than they are on our own—that this country succeeds when everyone gets a fair shot, everyone does their fair share, and everyone plays by the same rules. The Democratic Party is focused on building an economy that lifts up all Americans, not just those at the top.

Fight for $15
email: info@fightfor15.org
website: fightfor15.org

The Fight for $15 began in 2012 when two hundred fast-food workers walked off the job to demand $15/hr and union rights in New York City. Today, they are a global movement in over three hundred cities on six continents.

The International Socialist Organization
phone: (202) 643-8444
email: dc@internationalsocialist.org (Washington, DC branch)
website: www.internationalsocialist.org

The ISO is a US organization with branches and members in about forty cities and connections to other socialists around the world. It organizes in the here and now against injustice and for reforms that will benefit the working class and oppressed.

Occupy Wall Street
website: occupywallst.org

Occupy Wall Street is fighting back against the corrosive power of major banks and multinational corporations over the democratic process and the role of Wall Street in creating an economic collapse that has caused the greatest recession in generations. OccupyWallSt .org is the oldest and most trusted online resource for the Occupy movement, founded on July 14, 2011.

Republican National Committee
310 First Street SE
Washington, DC 20003
phone: (202) 863-8500
website: www.gop.com

The Republican National Committee provides national leadership for the Republican Party of the United States. The conservative party platform supports free market capitalism and free enterprise, a strong military, government deregulation, and socially conservative issues.

Bibliography

Books

Chip Berlet and Mathew N. Lyons. *Right Wing Populism in America: Too Close for Comfort*. New York, NY: Guilford Press, 2016.

Carlos de la Torre. *The Promise and Perils of Populism: Global Perspectives*. Lexington, KY: University Press of Kentucky, 2014.

John B. Judis. *The Populist Explosion: How the Great Recession Transformed American and European Politics*. New York, NY: Columbia Global Reports, 2014.

Michael Kazin. *The Populist Persuasion: An American History*. Ithaca, NY: Cornell University Press, 2014.

Benjamin Moffitt. *The Global Rise of Populism: Performance, Political Style, and Representation*. Palo Alto, CA: Stanford University Press, 2016.

Cas Mudde. *The Populist Radical Right: A Reader*. London and New York, NY: Routledge, 2016.

Cas Mudde and Cristobal Rovira Kaltwasser. *Populism: A Very Short Introduction*. New York, NY: Oxford University Press, 2017.

Jan-Werner Müller. *What Is Populism?* Philadelphia, PA: University of Pennsylvania Press, 2016

Periodicals and Internet Sources

Jahue Anderson, "Populism: Gender and Race in the Populist Party," Dr. Anderson's Blog, September 13, 2010. http://americanhistorytext.wordpress.com/2010/09/13/chapter-16-populism-and-gender-and-race-in-the-populist-party/.

John Emerson, "A Short History of Populism in America," CounterPunch, November 5, 2013. http://www.counterpunch.org/2013/11/05/a-short-history-of-populism-in-america/.

Jeet Heer, "Trump's Permanent Twitter Campaign," *New Republic*, December 1, 2016. http://newrepublic.com/article/139065/trumps-permanent-twitter-campaign.

Chris Lehmann, "Donald Trump and the Long Tradition of American Populism," *Newsweek*, August 22, 2015. http://www.newsweek.com/donald-trump-populism-365052.

Joe Lowndes and Dorian Warren, "Occupy Wall Street: A Twenty-First Century Populist Movement?" *Dissent Magazine*, October 21, 2011. https://www.dissentmagazine.org/online_articles/occupy-wall-street-a-twenty-first-century-populist-movement.

Santiago Zabala, "The Difference Between Right and Left-Wing Populism," Al Jazeera Media Network, January 17, 2017. http://www.aljazeera.com/indepth/opinion/2017/01/difference-left-wing-populism-170112162814894.html.

Index